Alex Pettes
Jan 2011

SACRED JOURNEY
OF THE
PEACEFUL
WARRIOR

Books by Dan Millman

THE PEACEFUL WARRIOR SAGA
Way of the Peaceful Warrior
Sacred Journey of the Peaceful Warrior

GUIDEBOOKS
Body Mind Mastery
Divine Intervention
Everyday Enlightenment
Living on Purpose
The Laws of Spirit
No Ordinary Moments
The Life You Were Born to Live

ESPECIALLY FOR CHILDREN
Secret of the Peaceful Warrior
Quest for the Crystal Castle

For information about Dan Millman's seminars,
please see the back pages of this book.

SACRED JOURNEY

OF THE

PEACEFUL
WARRIOR

DAN MILLMAN

H J KRAMER

NEW WORLD LIBRARY
NOVATO, CALIFORNIA

An H J Kramer Book
Published in a joint venture with
New World Library

Editorial office: Administrative office:
H J Kramer Inc.   New World Library
P. O. Box 1082   14 Pamaron Way
Tiburon, California 94920   Novato, California 94949

Editor: Nancy Grimley Carleton
Cover Design: Mary Ann Casler
Text Design and Typography: Cathey Flickinger
Cover Illustration: Terry Lamb

Library of Congress Cataloging-in-Publication Data
Millman, Dan.
Sacred journey of the peaceful warrior / Dan Millman.
p.   cm.
Sequel to: Way of the peaceful warrior.
ISBN 1-932073-10-8 (pbk.: alk. paper)
1. Spiritual life. 2. Millman, Dan. I. Title.
BL624.M5   1991
291.4′4 — dc20   91-11234
                                    CIP

Revised edition — First printing, May 2004
ISBN 1-932073-10-8
Printed in Canada on acid-free, partially recycled paper
Distributed to the trade by Publishers Group West

10   9   8   7   6   5

To my wife, Joy,
for her constant guidance and support,
and to my daughters, Holly, Sierra, and China,
who remind me about the important things.

To our readers:
The books we publish
are our contribution to an emerging world based on
cooperation rather than on competition,
on affirmation of the human spirit rather
than on self-doubt, and on the certainty
that all humanity is connected.
Our goal is to touch as many
lives as possible with a
message of hope for
a better world.

Hal and Linda Kramer, Publishers

CONTENTS

Book Three: The Great Leap

What if you slept, and what if in your sleep
you dreamed, and what if in your dream
you went to heaven and there you plucked a strange
and beautiful flower, and what if when you awoke
you had the flower in your hand? Oh, what then?

— Samuel Taylor Coleridge

MY FIRST BOOK, *Way of the Peaceful Warrior,* relates my adventures, training, and tests with an old service-station mechanic whom I named "Socrates." Readers of *Peaceful Warrior* will remember how, after expanding my view of life, he sent me away to assimilate his teachings and prepare myself for a final confrontation described at the end of that book.

This period of exile, preparation, and initiation that I am about to relate begins with personal struggles that send me on a quest to reawaken the faith I had found with Socrates, then somehow lost.

Sacred Journey stands alone, and it can be read independent of *Way of the Peaceful Warrior.* However, you should understand that this story takes place not after, but within *Peaceful Warrior.* In other words, you could read *Way of the Peaceful Warrior* to page 184, then read *Sacred Journey* in its entirety, and then read the rest of *Way of the Peaceful Warrior.* That's how the saga actually unfolds in chronological order. It is not necessary to read them this way, but at least now you understand where this story fits within the larger picture.

In the future I expect to write other books in this series. But now we turn to *Sacred Journey*.

I have, in fact, traveled around the world, had unusual experiences, and met remarkable people, but this book blends fact and fiction, weaving threads from the fabric of my life into a quilt that stretches across different levels of reality. By presenting spiritual teachings in story form, I hope to breathe new life into ancient wisdom, and to remind you that all our journeys are sacred, and all our lives an adventure.

A Suggestion from Socrates

> Free will does not mean that you establish the curriculum;
> only that you can elect what you want
> to take at a given time.
>
> — *A Course in Miracles*

LATE AT NIGHT in an old Texaco service station, during training sessions that ranged from meditation to cleaning toilets, from deep massage to changing spark plugs, Socrates would sometimes mention people or places I might someday visit for my "continuing education."

Once he spoke of a woman shaman in Hawaii. On other occasions, he referred to a school for warriors, hidden somewhere in Japan or China, and of a book or journal he had lost somewhere in the desert.

Naturally, these things intrigued me, but when I asked for details he would change the subject, so I was never certain whether the woman, the school, or the book actually existed.

In 1968, just before he sent me away, Socrates again spoke of the woman shaman. "I wrote to her about a year ago, and I mentioned you," he said. "She wrote back — said she might be willing to instruct you. Quite an honor," he added, and suggested that I look her up when the time felt right.

"Well, where do I find her?" I asked.

"She wrote the letter on bank stationery."

"What bank?" I asked.

"I don't recall. Somewhere in Honolulu, I think."

"Can I see the letter?"

"Don't have it anymore."

"Does she have a name?" I asked, exasperated.

"She's had several names. Don't know what she's using right now."

"Well, what does she look like?"

"Hard to say; I haven't seen her in years."

"Socrates, help me out here!"

With a wave of his hand, he said, "I've told you, Dan — I'm here to support you, not make it easy on you. If you can't find her, you're not ready anyway."

I took a deep breath and counted to ten. "Well what about those other people and places you mentioned?"

Socrates glared at me. "Do I look like a travel agent? Just follow your nose; trust your instincts. Find her first; then one thing will lead to the next."

Walking back toward my apartment in the silence of the early morning hours, I thought about what Socrates had told me — and what he hadn't: If I was "ever in the neighborhood," he had said, I might want to contact a nameless woman, with no address, who might still work at a bank somewhere in Honolulu; then again, she might not. If I found her, she might have something to teach me, and might direct me to the other people and places Socrates had spoken of.

As I lay in bed that night, a part of me wanted to head straight for the airport and catch a plane to Honolulu, but more immediate issues demanded my attention: I was about to compete for the last time in the NCAA Gymnastics Championships, then graduate from college and get married — hardly the best time to run off to Hawaii on a wild-goose chase. With that decision, I fell asleep — in a sense, for five years. And before I awakened, I was to discover that in spite of all my training and spiritual sophistication, I remained unprepared for what was to follow, as I leaped out of Soc's frying pan and into the fires of daily life.

— BOOK ONE —

Where Spirit Leads

The important thing is this:
To be ready at any moment
to sacrifice what you are
for what you could become.

— Charles Dubois

CHAPTER 1

Out of the Frying Pan

*Enlightenment consists not merely
in the seeing of luminous shapes and visions,
but in making the darkness visible.
The latter procedure is more difficult,
and therefore, unpopular.*

— Carl Jung

I WAS MARRIED on a Sunday in the spring of 1967, during my senior year at U.C. Berkeley. After a special dinner, Linda and I spent our brief honeymoon in a Berkeley hotel. I remember waking before dawn, unaccountably depressed. With the world still cloaked in darkness, I slipped out from under the rumpled covers and stepped softly out onto the balcony so as not to disturb Linda. As soon as I closed the sliding glass door, my chest began to heave and the tears came. I could not understand why I felt so sad, except for a troubling intuition that I had forgotten something important, and that my life had somehow gone awry. This sense would cast a shadow over the years to follow.

After graduation, I left the familiar college routine and my athletic career behind me. Linda was pregnant, so it was time for

3

me to grow up and find work. We moved to Los Angeles, where I sold life insurance. I felt as if I were inhabiting someone else's life. Then I learned that a coaching position had opened up at Stanford University. I applied for and got the job. We moved back to northern California; our daughter Holly was born. To all appearances I led a charmed life — so I continued to deny the feeling that something felt fundamentally wrong.

Four years passed. The Vietnam War. The moon landing. Watergate. Meanwhile, I immersed myself in the insular world of university politics, professional aspirations, and family responsibilities. My experiences with Socrates — and his words about the woman in Hawaii, the school in Japan, and some kind of book in the desert — faded into the dark recesses of my memory and then were lost in the shadows.

In 1972 I left Stanford to accept a faculty position at Oberlin College in Ohio, hoping that I might outrun my depression and strengthen our marriage. But these new surroundings only served to clarify our diverging values: Linda was at home in a conventional world that repelled me for reasons I couldn't explain. I envied her comfort. I looked at myself in the mirror of our relationship, and I didn't like what I saw. I had once viewed myself as a knight in shining armor. Now the armor had rusted. Even as I played the role of a wise college professor, I felt like a charlatan.

Despite Socrates' lessons about living in the present moment, my mind buzzed with regret and anxiety. I was no longer good company, not even for myself. Overstressed and out of shape, I lost my physical edge and self-respect. Even worse, I was going through the motions, having lost any sense of the deeper purpose or reason for my existence. I started to wonder: Could I continue to pretend that everything was well when my heart and guts told me something else? Would I have to pretend for the rest of my life?

Linda sensed my discontent, and we drifted further apart — she found other, more satisfying relationships, until the weakening thread that held us together finally snapped, and we decided to separate. I moved out on a cold day in March. The snow had turned to slush as I carried my few possessions to a friend's van and found a room in town. Lost and miserable, I didn't know where to turn.

A few weeks later, while glancing at a faculty newsletter, an item caught my eye: It was an invitation for interested faculty to apply for a travel grant to pursue "cross-cultural research." A sense of destiny coursed through me — I was certain that I was meant to do this. Two hours later I had completed the application. Three weeks later, I was awarded the grant. A window had opened; I had a direction once more, if only for the summer.

But where would I travel? The answer came during a yoga class I had joined to get back into some kind of shape. The breathing and meditative exercises reminded me of techniques I had learned from Joseph, one of Soc's students who had owned a small café in Berkeley before he died. Joseph had lived in Mysore, India, for a time, and had spoken positively of his experiences there. I had also read books on Indian saints, sages, and gurus, as well as on Vedantic philosophy. Surely, in India, I might rediscover that transcendent sense of freedom I had experienced with Socrates.

I would travel light, taking only a small backpack and an open airline ticket for maximum flexibility. I studied maps, did some research, and got a passport and immunizations. My plans made, I told Linda the news and explained that I would send our daughter postcards and would call when possible, but that I might be out of touch.

"That's nothing new," she said.

ON A WARM SPRING MORNING just before the school year ended, I sat on the lawn with my four-year-old daughter. "Sweetheart, I have to go away for a while."

"Where are you going, Daddy?"

"To India."

"Where they have elephants?"

"Yes."

"Can Mommy and me go with you?"

"Not this time, but someday we'll go on a trip together — just you and me. Okay?"

"Okay." She paused. "Which way is India?"

"That way," I pointed.

"Will you be gone a long time?"

"Not so very long. Just the summer — maybe a little longer. You'll have summer camp."

"But I won't have you. Who will read to me before I go to sleep?"

"Your mommy will."

"You're funnier. And why can't you move back home with us?"

I had no answer to that. I could only say, "Wherever I am, I'll be loving you and remembering you."

"Do you have to go, Daddy?"

It was a question I had asked myself many times. And answered. "Yes, I do."

She sat with this for a few moments. "Okay. Will summer camp be fun?"

"I expect it will."

"Will you send me postcards?"

"Whenever I can," I said, putting my arm around her. We sat this way for a while, and I think it made us both happy and sad at the same time.

A week later, the school year ended. After a bittersweet good-bye to Linda, I hugged my little daughter and slid into the taxi. "Hopkins Airport," I said to the driver. As we pulled away, I looked back through the rear window to see my familiar world growing smaller, until only my own reflection remained, staring back at me in the rear window. I had the summer to search, and to see what would unfold.

CHAPTER 2

The Journey

A ship is safe in harbor,
but that's not what ships are for.

— John A. Sheed

RESTING BETWEEN HEAVEN AND EARTH, I gazed out the window of the 747, down into the blanket of clouds covering the Indian Ocean, and I wondered if the answers I sought lay somewhere below. As I watched these thoughts float by, my eyelids slowly closed.

Moments later it seemed, I was startled awake as the jet's wheels touched down in the ancient land and bustling metropolis of Delhi. I had arrived in the humid monsoon season — constantly drenched by rain or sweat, I traveled by antique taxis, rickshaws, buses, and trains, then walked along muddy roads and through noisy bazaars where Hindu fakirs demonstrated unusual powers, disciplines, and austerities.

Days passed in dreamlike impressions of bright colors and strange scents as incense and cow dung blended in the oppressive heat. From Calcutta to Madras to Bombay, I moved among milling crowds. Sacred India, overburdened with bodies compressing into every square mile, every square foot, it seemed.

I found my way into numerous schools of yoga, where I learned a variety of postures, breathing systems, and meditations like those Socrates and Joseph had shown to me. In Calcutta, I saw the poorest of the poor, living in squalor. Everywhere I turned, I met beggars — men, women, crippled children in ragged clothing. Days later, in stark contrast to squalor, I stood on the bank of the Yamuna River in Agra, awestruck by the grandeur of the Taj Mahal and other temples of beauty and spiritual balance, as well as lesser-known ashrams potent with spiritual force.

On my pilgrimage I met sages speaking the ancient wisdom of Advaita Vedanta, a nondualistic philosophy which teaches that samsara and nirvana, flesh and spirit, are not separate, and whose holy trinity are Brahma the Creator, Vishnu the Sustainer, and Shiva the Destroyer. I also sat at the feet of gurus who spoke simple wisdom and emanated a loving and powerful presence. I felt the deep devotional fervor of the *bhakta,* of holy men and women. I trekked with Sherpa guides to Tibet, Nepal, breathing the rarefied air; I sat in caves and meditated.

But as the weeks passed, I grew more dejected, because I never found anyone like Socrates, nor did I learn anything that wasn't available in a West Coast bookstore. I felt as if I'd gone searching for the secrets of the East only to discover that the "East" had apparently moved to California.

I have the greatest respect for the spiritual traditions of India; I honor its cultural heritage and human treasures. But everywhere I went, I felt as if I were on the outside looking in, fishing in an empty pond. It wasn't India's failing; it was mine. After five weeks, disheartened but resolute, I decided to return home and try to put my broken family life back together. It was the right thing to do, the responsible thing. I would take the eastern route home, flying from India to Hawaii for a few days rest, then back to Ohio — to my wife and daughter. Somehow, I thought, things might still work out. Maybe coming up empty in India was a sign that my time with Socrates was all the spiritual training I was meant to have.

But if that were true, I thought, why is this restless feeling growing stronger?

The departing jet flew through the night, its wing lights flashing like tiny stars as we passed over a sleeping world. I tried to read but couldn't concentrate. I tried to sleep but dreams assailed me. Socrates' face kept popping up, along with fragments of things said long ago. By the time we landed in Hawaii, the "pay-attention-there's-something-you're-missing" feeling became intolerable, like a fire in my belly. I felt like screaming, What am I supposed to *do?*

As I CLEARED CUSTOMS and emerged, stretching, into the bright sun, the moist Hawaiian breezes soothed me, at least for the moment. Legend had it that these islands — born of earth, air, fire, and water — radiated a powerful healing energy long before sailors, priests, developers, and history opened Hawaii as a tourist attraction. I hoped that beneath the veneer of civilization some of the healing energy remained, and that it might quiet that barking dog inside me that wouldn't let up.

After a snack at the airport, a noisy bus ride through the busy streets of Waikiki, and an hour on foot, I found a small room off the beaten path. I tested the leaky toilet, then quickly unpacked the few belongings I'd stored in my old backpack. The half-open drawer of the nightstand revealed a dog-eared phone directory and a barely used Bible. It would do for a few days.

Suddenly tired, I lay back on the squeaky, sagging mattress, and I remembered nothing more — until my eyes snapped open and I jolted upright. "The woman shaman!" I yelled out loud, half-asleep, hardly knowing what I was saying. Then my brain awoke fully. "How could I have forgotten?" I pounded my forehead. "Think!" What had Socrates told me? First one memory surfaced, then another. He had urged me to find someone in Hawaii, and he had mentioned a school in — where was it? — Japan? China? And...something about a book or volume from a journal he had lost in the desert.

One day I might find that journal. But first I had to find the woman. Of course — *that's* why I'm here I realized; *that's* the sense of destiny that had been gnawing at my insides. Finally, I knew the real reason I'd taken this journey. It was as if I'd been wandering, lost in a forest, then stumbled back onto the path. Once this fell into place, my belly relaxed, and the ache changed to excitement. I could hardly contain my energy. My mind raced: What had he told me about the woman? She had written to him on some kind of stationery — *bank* stationery, that was it!

I grabbed the yellow pages and looked up "banks"; I counted twenty-two of them in Honolulu alone. "Who am I kidding?" I muttered to myself. He hadn't told me her name or address, or what she looked like. I had almost nothing to go on. It seemed impossible.

Then the sense of destiny filled me again. No, this couldn't all be for nothing. I was here, and somehow I would find her. I looked at my watch. If I rushed, I could check out a few banks before closing time.

But this was Hawaii, not New York City; people here didn't

rush anywhere. And what would I do at the first bank anyway —
walk in wearing a signboard that said, "Looking for someone special"? Would I whisper, "Socrates sent me" to every teller? I could
only hope that somehow this woman might recognize the name I
had given him — *if* she still worked at a bank, *if* she existed at all.

I stared out the window at a brick wall across the alley. The
beach was only ten blocks away; I'd get some dinner, go for a walk
in the sand, and decide what to do. I made it to the water's edge
just in time for sunset, only to realize that the sun set on the western side of the island, and I was on the eastern shore. "Terrific," I
said under my breath. "How am I going to find my mystery
woman if I can't even find the sunset?"

I lay down on the soft sand, still warm in the evening air, and
gazed up at a palm tree overhead. Watching its green fronds sway-
ing in the soft breeze, I searched through my mind for a plan.

The next day, as I walked by the office of a local newspaper, it
came to me. I entered the building, and quickly composed an ad
to appear in the "Personals" column. It read: "Young friend of
Socrates, seeking like-minded female banker. Let's make change
together." I added my motel phone number. Probably a lame idea,
with about the same odds of success as stuffing a note in a bottle
and tossing it into the sea. A long shot, but at least a chance.

SEVERAL DAYS PASSED. I visited art galleries, went snorkeling, and
lay on the beach — waiting, just waiting. My personal ad had
come up empty, and pounding the pavement seemed like an exercise in futility. Discouraged, I called the airport and booked a
flight home. I was ready to call it quits.

On the bus ride to the airport, I sat in a kind of stupor,
unaware of my surroundings. I found myself standing in front of
the airline counter. Then, in the boarding lounge, as the agent

called my flight, a voice inside me said, No. And I knew I couldn't give up. Not now, not ever. I had to find this woman, the link between my past and future.

I canceled my flight, bought a city map, and caught the next bus back to Honolulu. On the way, I marked the location of every bank on my list.

THE FIRST BANK, featuring generic bank decor, was nearly empty at this time of day. Scanning the room, I spotted a good possibility — a slender, athletic-looking woman, maybe in her late forties. She turned and gave me a brief smile. When our eyes met, I experienced a flash of intuition — this was incredible! Why hadn't I trusted myself from the start? She finished talking to one of the bank officers and returned to her desk by the safety deposit boxes and the vault. I waited patiently for the right moment; then, taking a deep breath, I walked up to her.

"Excuse me," I said, wearing my brightest, clearest, most alert smile so I wouldn't appear totally crazy. "I'm looking for a woman — no, let me rephrase that — I'm looking for someone who happens to be female, but I don't know her name. You see, an old gentleman — well, he's not exactly a gentleman — uh, an old man named Socrates suggested I find her. Does that name mean anything to you?"

"Socrates?" she said. "Isn't he a Greek or Roman guy — in history?"

"Yes, he is — was — " I answered, my hope dampened. "Maybe you don't know him by that name. He's a teacher of mine; I met him in a *gas station,*" I whispered emphatically, "a gas station in *California.*" Then I waited, and held my breath.

Slowly, her eyes grew wider and then a light went on. "Yes! I had a boyfriend once who worked in a station in California. But his name was Ralph. So you think it could have been Ralph?"

"Uh, no," I answered, disappointed. "I don't think so."

"Yeah, well, I gotta get back to work. I hope you find Archimedes — "

"Socrates," I corrected her. "And I'm not looking for him. I'm looking for a *woman!*"

I felt a chill, and her tone shifted. "Excuse me, please. I hope you find a woman soon."

I felt her gaze on the back of my neck as I walked over to another bank employee and did a variation of the same routine with a woman about fifty years old wearing heavy pancake makeup and rouge. Not a likely candidate, but I had to be thorough. She exchanged glances with the first teller, then looked back at me, her eyes filled with suspicion. "Can I help you?" she asked.

They must learn some kind of bank telepathy, I thought.

"I'm looking for a woman who works at the bank," I explained, "but I've misplaced her name. You wouldn't happen to know anyone named Socrates — "

"Perhaps you'd better talk to an officer," she interrupted. At first I thought she was referring to a security officer, but she pointed to a third woman in a dark suit, sitting behind a desk, just getting off the phone.

With a quick nod of thanks, I walked over to the officer, looked her in the eyes, and declared, "Hi, I'm a peaceful warrior looking for a friend of Socrates."

"What?" she replied, glancing toward the security guard.

"I said I'm a *potential customer looking for a fund of securities.*"

"Oh," she said, smiling and straightening her coat. "Then I think we can help you."

"Oh gosh, will you look at the time!" I said, looking at my watch. "I'll get back to you. We'll do lunch. Good-bye, ciao, cheers, aloha." I left.

I used the same peaceful warrior/potential customer line the rest of the afternoon. Then I found a bar and had my first beer in a long time. And I don't even like beer. As I walked through the crowded streets of downtown Honolulu, I thought about the woman, and realized she would have to be considerably older than forty or fifty or even sixty. If Socrates had really been in his nineties, as he claimed, she would have to be in her late seventies. Almost certainly retired, I thought, disheartened. Still, someone might know, might remember her.

Eight banks later, I sat against the wall of yet another institution of higher finance and reminded myself, Never, ever, even *think* about becoming a private investigator. My back ached and I felt like I was developing an ulcer. The whole thing seemed crazy. Maybe someone had given the woman the bank stationery. Why would a shaman work at a bank? But, then, why would an old warrior like Socrates choose to work at a gas station?

More confused and discouraged than ever, I had no more illusions about magically bumping into a shaman in a bank who would immediately recognize me as her prodigal son. Any remaining faith in my intuition was smashed as flat as the soda can near me on the sidewalk. I picked it up, stood, and tossed the can in the trash — a good deed. At least the entire day wouldn't be wasted.

The next day, I made the rounds at another ten banks until, exhausted and numb, I could do no more. I was asked to leave by the security guard at two savings and loans and almost got arrested at the last bank when I became belligerent. My nerves frazzled, I decided to call it a day.

That night, I dreamed I kept walking right past the woman I was seeking, narrowly missing her — like a scene in the movies when the two main characters are about to meet but turn their backs at the last minute and miss each other. This scene kept repeating itself in a maddening series of retakes.

I woke up tired. I was ready and willing to do *anything* that day — anything at all — except search for a nameless female bank employee. But somehow — and here my training with Socrates really paid off — I willed myself to get up, get dressed, and get going. Little disciplines like that can make all the difference in the world.

The following day tested my limits. I did find one bright spot, however, an oasis in a sea of frowning faces: At the fourth bank of the day, I met an extraordinarily pretty teller, about my age. When I told her I was looking for a *specific* woman, she asked, with a dimpled smile, "Am *I* specific enough?"

"I . . . uh . . . as a matter of fact, you are one of the most specific women I've seen in a long time." I grinned. I certainly doubted she was the woman shaman, but stranger things had happened, and with Socrates — well, you never knew.

She stared into my eyes, as if waiting for something. Maybe she was just flirting. Maybe she wanted me to make a deposit in her bank. Or maybe she knew something. For all I knew, she could be the shaman's daughter. Or something. I couldn't afford to pass up any lead, I told myself. Anyway, I could stand a little fun.

"Do you know who I am?" I asked.

"You look familiar," she answered.

Damn. Did she know or didn't she? "Look, uh," I glanced at her nameplate on the counter, "Barbara. My name's Dan; I'm a college professor visiting Honolulu, and well, it's kind of lonely, vacationing by yourself. I know we just met, but would you consider having dinner with me after work? Maybe you could show me where the sun sets, or we could talk about gas stations and old teachers."

She smiled again — definitely a good sign. "If that's a line," she said, "at least it's original. I get off at five; I'll meet you out front."

"Hey, that's terrific! See you then."

I walked out of the bank feeling good. I had a date, maybe even a lead. But then why did a little voice inside me say, "Idiot! What are you doing? Socrates sends you on a quest and you pick up a bank teller?"

"Oh, shut up!" I said aloud as a passerby turned and gave me a look.

My watch read 2:35. I could still make it to two, maybe three more banks before five o'clock. I looked at my street map, now speckled with crossed-out bank sites; the First Bank of Hawaii was right around the corner.

CHAPTER 3

Fool's Gold

When one is willing and eager, the gods join in.

— Aeschylus

As soon as I entered the lobby, the guard glanced in my direction, started toward me, then walked right by; I let out my breath and glanced up at the cameras; they all seemed focused on me. With a businesslike air, I walked over to a counter, pretended to fill out a deposit slip, and cased the joint.

A few feet away sat a functional desk, behind which sat a functional bank officer — a tall, aristocratic-looking woman in her fifties. She glanced up at me as I approached. But before I could ask her anything, she stood up. "I'm sorry — I'm taking a late lunch — but I think Mrs. Kaneoha can help you," she said, pointing back toward the other desk. Then she turned, and left.

"Uh, thanks," I mumbled after her.

Mrs. Kaneoha offered no help, nor did any of the other tellers or officers at that or the next bank, where I was helped outside by the security officer, who invited me not to come back.

Ready to laugh — or cry — I slumped against the last bank's polished stone exterior and slid to a sitting position on the sidewalk. "I've had it," I said out loud. "That's it, forget it, no more banks."

I understood the importance of persevering, but there's a point to stop banging your head against a wall. And this just wasn't working out. I would go on my date, watch the sun set, and then head back to Ohio.

As I sat there feeling sorry for myself, I heard a voice ask, "Are you all right?" I looked up to see a small but plump Asian woman with silver hair, wearing an oversized muumuu, holding a bamboo cane. She looked about seventy years old — maybe older. She smiled down at me with an expression of maternal concern.

"I'm okay, thanks," I replied, standing up with some effort.

"You don't look okay," she said. "You look tired."

Irritable, I almost snapped, What business is it of yours? But I took a deep breath instead. "You're right," I confessed. "I am tired. But I've been tired before; I'll be fine, thanks." I expected her to nod and walk away, but she stood there, staring at me.

"Just the same," she said, "I'll bet you could use a glass of juice."

"Are you a doctor or something?" I asked, half in fun.

"No," she smiled. "Not really. But Victor — my godson — he burns it at both ends, too." Seeing my puzzled look, she quickly added, "You know, his candle."

"Oh," I replied, smiling. She seemed like a nice lady. "Well, I guess I could stand a glass of juice. Can I get you one, too?"

"That's very nice of you," she said as we entered a sidewalk café next door to the bank. I noticed she walked with a pronounced limp.

"My name's Ruth Johnson," she informed me, leaning her old bamboo cane against the counter and reaching out to shake hands. Johnson — it wasn't your typical Asian surname; I guessed she was married to a Caucasian.

"Dan Millman," I said in return, shaking her hand. I ordered a carrot juice.

"The same," said Mrs. Johnson. As she turned her head toward the waitress, I studied her face — part Hawaiian, I guessed, or maybe Japanese or Chinese, with an overlay of tan.

The waitress set our juices down on the counter. I picked mine up, then noticed Mrs. Johnson staring at me. Her eyes caught mine, and held them. She had deep eyes, like Socrates. Oh, come *on,* I thought. Stop imagining things.

She continued to stare. "Do I know you from somewhere?"

"I don't think so," I said. "This is my first time here."

"In Honolulu?"

No, on planet earth, I thought. "Yes," I said aloud.

She examined me intently for another moment, then remarked, "Well, then, it must be my imagination. So, you're visiting?"

"Yes, I'm on the faculty at Oberlin College — here on a research trip," I replied.

"No, go on! Oberlin? One of my nieces went to Oberlin!"

"Oh, really," I said, looking at my watch.

"Yes. And my godson, Victor — he's considering it for next year. He just graduated from Punaho School. Say, why don't you come over to the house tonight? You could meet Victor; he'd be *thrilled* to talk with an Oberlin professor!"

"I appreciate the invitation, but I have other plans."

Not at all discouraged, but with a trembling hand, she scrawled an address on a piece of paper and handed it to me. "If you change your mind."

"Thanks again," I said, standing to leave.

"Thank *you,*" she said, "for the juice."

"My pleasure," I answered, tossing a five-dollar bill on the counter. I hesitated for a moment, then asked, "You don't happen to work in a bank, do you?"

"No," she answered. "Why?"

"Oh, it's nothing."

"Well then, aloha," she waved. "Create a nice day."

I stopped and turned back toward her. "What was that you said — '*Create* a nice day'?"

"Yes."

"Well, most people say, '*Have* a nice day.'"

"I suppose they do."

"It's just that an old teacher of mine — he used to say that."

"Really," she nodded, smiling at me in a funny kind of way. "How interesting."

My reality meter started buzzing; my tongue went a little numb. Was something a little off?

She stared at me again, then impaled me with a look so intense the café disappeared. "I know you," she said.

Suddenly, everything grew brighter. I felt my face flush, and my hands started to tingle. Where had I last felt like this? Then I remembered. An old gas station, one starry night.

"You know me?"

"Yes. I wasn't sure at first, but now I recognize you as a good-hearted person, but I think a little hard on yourself."

"That's it?" I said, let down. "That's what you meant?"

"And I can tell that you're lonely, and that you need to relax a little more. A barefoot walk in the surf would relax you — yes, you need a barefoot walk in the surf," she whispered.

Dazed, I hear myself ask, "A barefoot walk in the surf?"

"Exactly."

In a fog, I started toward the exit, when I heard her say, "See you tonight — about seven o'clock."

I DON'T CLEARLY REMEMBER leaving the café. The next thing I knew, I found myself carrying my shoes, walking along the clean, wet sand of Waikiki, my feet washed by the shallow surf.

Some time later, a seagull landed nearby. I glanced at it, then suddenly looked up and around as if waking up. *What was I doing here?* In a moment it came back to me: Ruth Johnson... the café...her house...seven o'clock. I looked at my watch; it said 6:15.

A quarter after six, a quarter after six, I repeated to myself, as if that meant something. Then it dawned on me: I had just stood up Barbara, the pretty bank teller.

I felt pretty, too — pretty dense.

And so, with nothing else to do, I caught a bus to an attractive suburb of Honolulu, then walked until I found the address Ruth Johnson had written down. At least I thought I had found the right address; her handwriting wasn't very clear.

At 7:15, I walked up the driveway of a well-kept home. Cars filled the driveway, dance music poured out of the open doorway, and an older woman sat on a porch swing, gliding in and out of the moonlight. I climbed the steps and saw that she wasn't Ruth Johnson. Inside I heard people talking loudly. Someone laughed. I had a sinking feeling that this was the wrong place.

The woman on the swing said, "Aloha! Go on in!"

I nodded to her and entered the house, surveying the large living room, crowded with teenagers and a few older men and women — dancing, talking, eating — the women in flowered dresses or halter tops, and the men in jeans, T-shirts, and tank tops.

The music stopped for a moment; I heard a splash as someone jumped, or fell, into the swimming pool just visible through sliding doors. Loud laughter followed.

I tapped a young woman on the shoulder just as a rock-'n'-roll tune started; I had to yell to be heard above the music. "I'm looking for Ruth Johnson."

"Who?" she yelled back.

"Ruth Johnson!" I yelled louder.

"I don't know too many people here," she shrugged. "Hey, Janet," she called to someone else. "You know any Ruth Johnson?"

Janet said something I couldn't hear. "Never mind," I said, and headed for the door.

Walking down the front steps, I stopped, and gave it one last try. Turning to the woman on the swing, I asked, "Does Ruth Johnson live here?"

"No," she said.

"Oh." Depressed, I turned to leave. Couldn't I do *anything* right?

"Ruthie's staying with her sister down the street," the woman added. "She went to buy more soda."

Just then, a car pulled up in front.

"There she is now," the woman pointed.

No one got out of the car at first. Then I saw Ruth Johnson climb slowly to her feet. I quickly ran down the steps to meet her, anxious to get to the bottom of all this, one way or the other.

She was reaching to pick up a grocery bag when I said from behind her, "Let me help you with that." She turned and looked delighted — but not surprised — to see me.

"*Mahalo!* Thank you!" she said. "You see, I was right about your being a kind person."

"Maybe not as kind as you think," I said, as a picture of my young daughter, and the wife I'd left behind, flashed through my mind.

I walked slowly up the front steps to keep pace with her. "So, why did you really invite me here?" I asked.

"Sorry to slow you down," she said, ignoring my question. "I had a small — well, stroke, you could say. But I'm getting better all the time."

"Mrs. Johnson, can we get to the point?"

"I'm glad you found the house," she said.

"I've come a long way — "

"Yes, people come from all over for one of our parties. We really know how to have a good time!"

"You don't really know who I am."

"I don't imagine anyone really knows who anyone really is. But here we are anyway," she said brightly. "And while you're here, why don't you come in, meet Victor, and enjoy the party?"

Disappointed, I leaned up against the wall and stared at the ground.

"Are you all right?" she asked, concerned.

"I'm okay."

"Hey, Ruthie," someone yelled from inside. "Did you bring the soda and chips?"

"Have them right here, Bill."

She turned to me. "Uh, what did you say your name was?"

I looked up at her. "Dan." It came out like "damn."

"Well, Dan, come on in, dance a little, meet some people. That should perk you up."

"Look, I appreciate the offer — you seem like a nice lady — but I'd better be going; I have a lot to do tomorrow." Suddenly tired, I took a deep breath and stood. "Have a nice party, and thanks — uh, mahalo — for your kindness." I turned toward the street.

"Wait a moment," she said, limping after me. "Look, it was my mistake, having you come all the way out here. Let me give you something for the road." She reached into her purse.

"No, really, I couldn't. I don't need — "

She grabbed my hand and looked me in the eyes; the world started spinning. "You take this," she said, pushing what looked like crumpled bills into my hand. "Maybe we'll meet again."

She turned abruptly and entered the house. The sound of music grew louder, then suddenly quiet as the door slammed shut.

Clenching the money in my fist, I shoved it into my pocket and walked on, into the warm night.

Coconut and banyan trees and landscaped lawns faintly shone under the light of the street lamp near a bus stop, where I collapsed to a sitting position, trying to clear my head. Something was off here; nothing made sense. It *had* to be her, but it wasn't. I was back to zero.

I didn't know if I could bring myself to visit another bank; I was tired of getting treated like a nut case. Maybe it was hopeless; maybe I was just a strange person, as my wife had said. Maybe she was right about everything. Why couldn't I just be a normal guy and go to ball games and movies and have barbecues on Sunday?

I was seriously considering flying home the next day and seeing a good therapist when the bus arrived with a sighing of air brakes. The door opened; I got to my feet and reached into my pocket for the money — and saw that Ruth Johnson hadn't given me any money after all.

"Hey, buddy," the bus driver said. "You getting on or not?"

Intent on opening the crinkled pieces of paper, I hardly heard him, and didn't answer. Then my eyes opened wide and I stopped breathing. Vaguely aware of the bus pulling away without me, I stared at the two pieces of paper in my hands: The first was a newspaper ad, clipped from the "Personals" section. It began,

"Young peaceful warrior, friend of Socrates." I heard myself breathing rapidly; my whole body trembled.

On the second piece of paper, I found a note Mrs. Johnson had scrawled in a shaky, nearly illegible hand. It read:

I'm from the old school — the hard school. Nothing is given without desire, preparation, and initiation. There is a question of trust, and faith. On Thursday evening, three nights from now, the currents will be exactly right. If you wish to continue, follow all these instructions precisely: Go to Makapuu Beach in the early evening.

I turned the note over. It continued:

You will see a rocky area toward Makapuu Point. Walk toward the point until you find a small shed. One side is caved in. Behind it, you'll see a large surfboard. When you are alone — at dusk, not before — take the board and paddle out beyond the surf. A strong tide will be going out; let the currents take you. Be sure...

Strange — that was all. "Be sure..." The note ended there. What did she mean by that? I wondered, stuffing the note back into my pocket.

Then my wonder changed to excitement and a profound sense of relief. My search was over. I'd found her! A fountain of energy welled up inside me. My senses opened; I felt the temperature of the air, heard faraway crickets, and smelled the fresh aroma of newly mowed lawns, wet from an earlier rain. I walked all the way back to my motel. By the time I arrived, it was nearly dawn.

I fell onto the bed with a bounce and a squeak and stared at the ceiling. Much later, I drifted to sleep.

That night, I dreamed of skeletons — hundreds of them — bleached white by the sun, washed up on the rocky shore, lying askew on black lava rock. A wave crashed, and the shore was washed clean, leaving only the lava, black as night. The blackness swallowed me. I heard a roar, soft at first, then growing louder.

Awakened by the whine of a garbage truck outside, I opened my eyes and stared at the ceiling — but the stark images of skeletons remained in my mind, along with a sense of awe and foreboding. Thursday evening, it would begin.

THINGS WERE PICKING UP; a new wave was rising. Just like the old days. This intensity and excitement made me realize how sleepy my life had felt these past few years: I had become an armchair warrior whose battles were championed by alter egos on television or at the movies. Now I was on my own feet, waiting for the bell.

CHAPTER 4

A Fire at Sea

What is to give light must endure burning.

— Viktor Frankl

I HAD MADE NO SPECIAL PREPARATIONS, because apparently none were called for — just find a big surfboard and go for a paddle.

Thursday afternoon, I checked out of my hotel, ready to camp on the beach, ready for a change, ready for anything. Or so I thought. I carried my belongings, stuffed into my backpack, down to Makapuu Beach. Breathing in the fresh, salty air, I walked toward the point. In the distance ahead, atop a mound of lava rock, I saw an old lighthouse standing starkly against a crimson sky.

The walk was farther than I'd thought; it was nearly dark before I found the shed. The surfboard was there, just as she'd said. It wasn't the streamlined fiberglass I'd expected, but a massive, old-fashioned slab of wood, like the boards used by the ancient Hawaiian kings — I'd seen a picture of one in *National Geographic*.

I looked out over the deserted beach and calm ocean. In spite of the setting sun, the balmy air was comfortable. I stripped to my nylon trunks, stuffed my clothing and wallet into my pack, and hid my pack in the bushes. Then I carried the heavy board out into thigh-deep surf and set it down with a loud slap on the glassy surface.

With a last look down the beach, I pushed off, glided out, and paddled awkwardly through the waves. Panting with exertion, I finally broke through the last phosphorescent whitecap, barely illuminated by a waning moon that appeared and disappeared with passing clouds. Resting on the ocean's gentle rise and fall, I wondered about this strange initiation. Pleasant enough in the tropical sea, but how long did Ruth Johnson want me to float out here before coming back in. All night?

The rhythmic ocean swells soothed me into a pleasant lassitude. I lay on my back and gazed up into the constellations of Scorpio and Sagittarius. My eyes scanned the heavens and my thoughts drifted with the current as I waited for who knows what — maybe further instructions from a spaceship for all I knew.

I MUST HAVE FALLEN ASLEEP. I sat up, waking with a gasp, not knowing where I was. I found myself straddling the board as it rocked with the swells. Until I awoke, I hadn't realized that I'd been asleep. I wondered if enlightenment was like that.

I was looking around, trying to make out the coastline in the darkness when it struck me: the current. She had written something about the current being "exactly right." For what? I scanned the horizon in every direction, but with the sea's rise and fall, and the cloud cover, I was effectively blind until dawn; I saw no stars, no land.

I had left my watch on shore and had no sense of time or bearings. How long had I drifted? And where? With a chill, I realized I might be drifting straight out to sea. Gripped by a sudden panic, I forced myself to calm my breathing. Paranoid fantasies played in the theater of my imagination: What if this old woman is an eccentric, or even crazy? What if she has a score to settle with Socrates? Would she deliberately…? No, it couldn't be, I thought. But I had no certainty, no reference points. My usual methods of reality testing weren't helping me here.

As soon as I fought off one wave of fear, another would roll in. My mind sank beneath the surface, and I shuddered as I imagined monstrous shadows swimming beneath me. I felt small and alone, a floating speck in the ocean, a thousand feet above the ocean floor.

Hours passed, as far as I could reckon. I lay still, listening for the sound of a Coast Guard boat, scanning the heavens for signs of a rescue copter. But no one knew where I was — no one except Ruth Johnson.

The clouds blotted out the moon and stars, leaving the sky so dark I couldn't tell whether my eyes were open or closed. I drifted in and out of consciousness, afraid to sleep. But the gentle, lullaby rise and fall of the ocean swells won out, and I plunged down, slowly, into silence, like a rock sinking into the depths of the sea.

I AWOKE WITH THE FIRST LIGHT OF DAWN, realized where I was, sat up suddenly, and fell off the board. Sputtering and spitting out saltwater, I climbed back on the board and looked around with rising apprehension. I saw nothing but ocean; the clouds still obscured any sight of land. For all I knew, I was far out in the Pacific. I had heard about strong currents that could pull someone straight out to sea. I could paddle, but in what direction? Again fighting off panic, I forced myself to take another deep breath and tried to relax.

Then an even more disturbing revelation dawned on me: I had no shirt or sunscreen, no food, no water. For the first time, it occurred to me that I might really die out here — that this was no middle-class adventure. I might have made a very big mistake.

Ruth Johnson had written that it was "a question of trust and faith."

"Yeah," I muttered to myself, "trust, faith, and blind stupidity." What had possessed me? I mean, who takes a surfboard out into the ocean currents at night because an old woman writes him a note?

"This can't be happening," I said aloud, startled by the sound of my own voice, quickly drowned by the vast spaces above and below. I could already feel the heat of the morning sun on my back.

The clouds dissipated, leaving a burning azure sky. I had time to consider my situation — nothing but time. Except for the occasional call of an albatross or the faint drone of an airplane far above, silence was my only companion.

Once in a while, I splashed my feet in the salty water, or hummed a tune to reassure my ears. But soon enough, the tunes died. A sense of dread crept slowly up my spine.

As the day wore on, I grew thirsty, and my fear intensified with the heat of the sun. It wasn't the sudden fear of a gun in my ribs or a car weaving head-on into my lane — just a quiet kind of knowingness, a stark inevitability that unless someone rescued me soon, I would burn to death on the cool green sea.

The hours passed with agonizing slowness, and my skin started turning pink. By the late afternoon, thirst became an obsession. I tried everything I could think of to protect myself: I paddled the board around to face different directions; I slipped into the cooling water many times, under the shelter of the board, careful to maintain my hold on its cracked surface. The water was my only protection from the sun and carried me into the blessed dark.

All night, my body burned with fever, then shook with chills. Even the slightest movement felt painful. I shivered as I hugged myself, overcome with remorse. Why had I done such a foolish thing? How could I have trusted that old woman, and why would she have done this to me? Was she cruel, or merely mistaken? Either way, the outcome was the same: I would die without ever knowing why. *Why?* I asked myself again and again as my mind clouded over.

WHEN MORNING CAME, I lay still, my skin blistered and my lips cracked. I think I would have died, but for a gift from the sky: Dark clouds appeared with the dawn, and a rainstorm swept over, giving me a few hours of shade, and of life. Raindrops, mixed with tears of gratitude, stung my blistered face.

I had nothing to hold the water save my open mouth. I lay back with my jaws wide, trying to catch every drop, until my muscles began to spasm. I removed my trunks so they could soak up every possible bit of rainwater.

Too soon, the scorching sun returned, rising higher in the empty blue sky, as if the storm had never happened. My lips cracked into deep fissures. Surrounded by water, I was dying of thirst.

Mahatma Gandhi once said, "To a starving man, God is bread." Now, water had become my god, my goddess, my one thought and one passion — not enlightenment, not understanding — I would have traded them in an instant for one glass of pure, cool, quenching water.

I stayed in the water, clinging to the board, for most of the morning. But it did nothing for the horrible thirst. Later, in the afternoon, I thought I saw a dorsal fin circling nearby, and I quickly scrambled back onto the board. But as my skin blistered and I grew more parched, the thought entered my mind that a shark's jaws might be my only deliverance from slow death. Like a deer that bares its throat to the lion, a small but growing part of me wanted to give in, to just slip into the sea and disappear.

When night came again, I again burned with fever. In my delirium, I dreamed of swimming in a mountain spring, drinking my fill, lying in a calm pool, and letting the water seep into my pores. Then the smiling face of Ruth Johnson appeared, with her silver hair, her deep eyes mocking my foolishness.

Drifting in and out of consciousness with the rise and fall of the sea, my rational mind faded in, then out, like a ghost presence. In a lucid moment, I knew that if I didn't find land by the next day, it would be over.

Pictures flashed by: home in Ohio, in my backyard, sitting back in my lounge chair in the shade of a birch tree sipping a lemonade, reading a novel, playing with my daughter, eating a snack just because I was a little hungry — the comforts and safety of home. Now, all that seemed a far-off dream, and this, a nightmarish reality. If I slept at all, I don't remember.

Morning came much too soon.

That day I learned about hell: pain and burning, fear and waiting. I was ready to slip off the board and swim away in the cool water, to let Death take me — anything to stop the pain. I cursed the body, this mortal body. It was a burden now, a source of suffering. But another part of me hung on, determined to fight to my last breath.

The sun moved with agonizing slowness across the sky. I learned to hate the clear blue, and I gave silent thanks for every cloud that covered the sun as I clung to the board, submerged in the water I could not drink.

I lay exhausted through the next night — neither awake nor asleep — floating in purgatory. Squinting through swollen lids, I saw a vision of cliffs in the distance, and imagined I heard the faint pounding of surf against the rocks. Then, suddenly alert, I realized it was no vision. It was real. Hope lay ahead, and life. I was going to survive. I started to cry, but found I had no tears left.

A surge of energy coursed through me; my mind, now crystal clear, snapped into focus. I couldn't die now — I was too close! With all my remaining strength, I started paddling toward shore. I was going to *live*.

The cliffs now towered above me like gigantic skyscrapers, dropping straight down to the sea. With increasing speed, driven by the surf, I moved toward the rocks. Abruptly, the surf turned angry. I remember grabbing for my board as it snapped into the air and came crashing down. Then I must have passed out.

CHAPTER 5

New Beginnings

Healing is a matter of time,
but sometimes also a matter of opportunity.

— Hippocrates, *Precepts,* Chapter 1

ON THE ISLAND OF MOLOKAI, in Pelekunu Valley, set deep among moss-covered crags, lay a small cabin. Inside that cabin, a woman's screams pierced the air. "Mama Chia!* Mama Chia!" she cried out in pain and fear as she struggled in the throes of a difficult childbirth.

MOLOKAI — where, in the 1800s, the lepers had been exiled, left to die, isolated from the rest of the world by fear and ignorance.

Molokai — home of native Hawaiians, Japanese, Chinese, and Filipinos, with a small American and European population; a retreat for counterculture and alternative lifestyles; home of hardy, independent folk who avoid development and the tourist trade of the other islands, who work hard and live simply, who teach their children basic values and love of nature.

---

*Chia is pronounced "Chee-ah."

Molokai — island of nature spirits and legend, secret burial place of the *kahuna kupuas,* the shamans, magicians, and healers, the spiritual warriors attuned to the energies of the earth.

Molokai was ready to welcome another soul to the earth.

MITSU FUJIMOTO, a small Japanese American in her early forties, tossed her head from side to side, soaked in sweat. She prayed and moaned and cried for her child, calling weakly, "Mama Chia!" Pushing on, panting with each contraction, she fought for her baby's life.

HOURS OR MINUTES LATER — I couldn't tell — after drifting, delirious, in and out of consciousness, I awoke, desperately thirsty. If I felt thirsty, I was alive! The logic of that realization shocked me to my senses and, for a few rational moments, I scanned my body, taking stock inside and out. My head throbbed; my skin burned. And I couldn't see; I was blind! I moved my arm, now incredibly weak, and felt my eyes, discovering with great relief that they were covered with gauze.

I had no idea where I was — in a hospital, in a room, in Ohio, or maybe back in California. Maybe I had been ill or in some kind of accident. Or maybe it was all a dream.

MITSU'S LONG BLACK HAIR lay tangled and matted across her face and pillow. After her first child had died, nearly ten years before, she had vowed never to have another; she couldn't live through the pain of another such loss.

But when she passed the age of forty, she knew that this would be her last chance. It was now or never. So Mitsu Fujimoto and her husband, Sei, made their decision.

After many months, Mitsu's face grew radiant, and her belly ripe. The Fujimotos were to be blessed with a child.

Sei had run into the valley to find help. Now Mitsu lay contorted on her mattress, panting and resting between contractions — exhausted, alone, and afraid that something was terribly wrong, that the baby was turned around. As each tidal wave of contractions hardened her uterine wall like stone, Mitsu screamed again for Mama Chia.

WHEN I REGAINED CONSCIOUSNESS, the world remained dark, my eyes still covered with gauze. My skin was on fire; all I could do was moan, and bear it.

I heard a sound — what was it? — like someone wringing out a wet cloth over a bowl of water. As if in answer, a cool cloth touched my forehead; then a soothing odor filled my nostrils.

Me emotions very close to the surface, I felt a tear run down my cheek. "Thank you," I muttered, my scratchy voice barely audible.

I reached up slowly and clasped the small hand that held the cloth, now cooling my chest and shoulders.

I was surprised by the voice of a girl — a young girl, maybe nine or ten years old. "Rest now" was all she said.

"Thank you," I said again, then asked, "Water... please."

The girl's hand, behind my neck, gently lifted my head so I could drink. I grabbed the cup and poured more, until it spilled over my lips and down my chest. She pulled the cup back. "I'm sorry; I'm only supposed to let you sip a little at a time," she apologized, letting my head back down. Then, I must have slept.

MITSU'S PAIN CONTINUED, but she was now too exhausted to push, too weary to call out. Suddenly, the front door opened, and her husband rushed in, panting from the exertion of the steep dirt road. "Mitsu!" he called, "I've brought her!"

"Fuji, I need clean sheets — now." Mama Chia said, going straight to the exhausted mother-to-be and checking her vital signs. Then she quickly scrubbed her hands. "I'll need three clean towels as well — and boil a gallon of water. Then run back down to the truck and bring the oxygen."

Working quickly and efficiently, Mama Chia — midwife, healer, kahuna — again checked Mitsu's vital signs, and prepared to turn the baby. This might be a difficult birthing, but God willing, and with the help of the island spirits, she would save the mother and, together, they would bring a new life into the world.

THE BURNING HAD SUBSIDED from incessant pain to a mild throbbing. I tried, cautiously, to move the muscles of my face.

"What have I done to myself?" I asked in despair, still hoping to awaken from this nightmare — crazy, stupid, unnecessary. But it wasn't a dream. Tears stung my eyes. So weak I could hardly move, my mouth cracked and dry, I could barely mouth the words again, "Water...please." But no one heard.

I remembered something Socrates had told me about the search for ultimate meaning. "Better never to begin...but once begun...better finish."

"Better never begin..." I muttered, before dropping off to sleep.

THE CRY OF THE INFANT BOY resounded through the open windows of that tiny cabin in the rain forest. Mitsu managed a smile as she held the child to her breast. Fuji sat nearby, beaming, touching his wife, then his baby. Tears of joy ran down his cheeks.

Mama Chia cleaned up, as she had done many times in the past. "Mitsu and your son are going to be fine, Fuji. I'll leave them in your care now — and, I'm sure, in very good hands." She smiled.

He cried unabashedly, taking both her hands in his and lapsing from Hawaiian to Japanese to English: "Mama Chia, mahalo! Mahalo! *Arigato gozaimasu!* How can we ever thank you?" he asked, his eyes still wet with tears.

"You just did," she answered. But his expression told her that neither his thanks nor his tears would be adequate payment in Fuji's eyes — it was a matter of pride and honor — so she added, "I'd love some vegetables when you harvest. You grow the best yams on the island."

"You'll get the best of the best," he promised.

With a last look at Mitsu's tired but radiant face as she nursed her baby, Mama Chia gathered her backpack and left for her slow hike down into the valley. She had another patient to see.

I AWOKE AS THE SMALL, now familiar hands lifted my head and gently poured some liquid onto my tongue. I sucked it down greedily; it tasted strange, but good. After a few more sips, the hands carefully smoothed some kind of salve over my face, and then over my chest and arms.

"This is a poultice made from the fruit of the noni tree, mixed with aloe," she said in her soft young voice. "It will help your skin heal."

When I next awoke, I felt better. My headache was nearly gone, and my skin, though it felt tight, no longer burned. I opened my eyes; the gauze bandages were gone. Glad to have my sight once again, I turned my head slowly and looked around: I was alone, on a cot, in the corner of a small, but clean, one-room cabin built of logs. Light poured in through makeshift shades. A wooden chest sat at the foot of the bed. A chest of drawers stood against the far wall.

Many questions passed through my mind: Where am I? I asked myself. Who saved me? Who brought me here?

"Hello?" I said. "Hello?" I repeated louder. I heard footsteps, then a young girl entered. She had jet black hair and a beautiful smile.

"Hello," she said. "Are you feeling any better?"

"Yes," I answered. "Who... who are you? Where am I?

"You're *here,*" she answered amused. "And I am Sachi, Mama Chia's assistant," she said proudly. "My real name's Sachiko, but Mama Chia calls me Sachi for short — "

"Who is Mama Chia?" I interrupted.

"She's my auntie. She's teaching me about the kahuna ways."

"Kahuna — then I'm still in Hawaii?"

"Yes," she said, pointing to a faded map of the Hawaiian Islands on the wall behind my head. "This is Molokai."

Incredulous, I could only repeat the word. "Molokai? I drifted to *Molokai?*"

MAMA CHIA made her way slowly down the winding path. It had been a busy week, and these past few days had left her tired. But her work called forth an energy beyond that of her physical body.

She continued down the path through the forest. No time to rest now; she wanted to check on her new patient. Her flowered dress, still damp from a rain shower, bore spots of mud on its lower border. Her hair clung to her forehead in wet strands. Unconcerned about her appearance, she quickened her pace the best she could on the slippery forest trail on the way to her patient.

She turned a final bend in the path — her body remembering it so well she could walk it on a moonless night — and saw the small clearing and the cabin nestled, almost hidden, against a green wall of trees. "Just where I left it," she joked to herself. She passed the nearby storage shed and vegetable garden, and entered.

I TRIED SITTING UP and looking out the open window. The late afternoon sun slanted in and lit the opposite wall. Feeling woozy, I lay back down. "Sachi," I asked weakly, "how did I get here? And — "

Then, with a shock, I sat up again, and nearly passed out as a woman limped into the room and turned around.

"Ruth Johnson?" I said through cracked lips. I tried to sit up then thought better of it. This was no dream; the pain was real. The woman who had sent me out on the surfboard was standing over me now.

"You almost killed me!" I yelled.

The old woman set her cane against the wall, fluffed up my pillow, and gently pushed me back on the bed. She wasn't smiling, but her face had a tenderness I hadn't seen before. She turned to the young girl. "You've done a good job taking care of him, Sachi; your parents will be pleased."

Sachi smiled and left us alone.

"Who *are* you?" I asked the woman. *"What's going on here?"*

She didn't answer right away, but as she massaged another salve into the skin of my face, she said quietly, "I don't understand — you don't seem like a foolish young man — why did you ignore my directions? Why did you go out without any sunscreen, or food, or water?"

I pushed her hand away from my face and sat up again. *"What* directions? Why would I need sunscreen at night? Who takes food and water out on a surfboard? Why didn't you tell me what I would need?"

"But I *did* tell you," she interrupted. "I wrote it down — told you to be sure to take three days' supply of water, food, and sunscreen, and — "

"There was nothing about any of that in your note," I interrupted.

She paused, puzzled and thoughtful. "How can that be?" she asked, staring into space. "On the second page I wrote down everything — "

"What do you mean, 'second page'?" I asked. "All you gave me was the newspaper clipping, and a note. You wrote on the front and back — "

"But there was another page!" she said, cutting me off.

Then it dawned on me: "The note," I said, "It ended with the words, 'Be sure...' I thought you were just telling me to be certain."

As she realized what must have happened, Mama Chia closed her eyes; a mixture of emotions passed over her face for a moment, then disappeared. Shaking her head sadly, she sighed. "The next page told you everything you'd need and where the currents would take you."

"I — I must have dropped the other page when I was putting the papers in my pocket."

I lay back against the pillows. I didn't know whether to laugh or cry. "And I assumed, out there on the ocean that you were just from 'the hard school.'"

"Not that hard!" she replied. We laughed, because there was nothing else to do, and because the whole thing was so ludicrous.

Still laughing, she added, "And when you're feeling stronger, to finish the job, we can throw you off a cliff."

I laughed even louder than she; it made my head hurt again. And, just for a moment, I wasn't sure whether or not she was serious.

"But who are you? I mean — "

"On Oahu, I was Ruth Johnson. Here, my friends, students, patients — and people I've almost killed — call me Mama Chia." She smiled.

"Well, Mama Chia, how did I get here?"

She walked over to the island map and pointed: "The currents took you across the Kaiwi Channel, around Ilio Point, and eastward along the north shore of Molokai, past Kahiu Point, toward Kamakou, and you landed — ungracefully, I might add, but right on time — at Pelekunu Valley, just as I knew you would. There is a trail, a stairwell known by few people. Some friends helped carry you here."

"Where are we?"

"In a secluded place — a forest reserve."

I shook my head, then winced as it throbbed. "I don't understand any of this. Why all the mystery?"

"All part of your initiation — I told you. If you had been prepared..." Her words trailed off. "I acted carelessly. I'm sorry for what you had to endure, Dan. I intended to give you a test of faith, not get you deep-fried," she apologized again. "But like Socrates, I suppose I have a flair for the dramatic."

"Well," I said, "can I at least consider myself initiated?"

She sighed. "I should hope so."

After a pause, I asked, "How did you know I was coming to Hawaii? Until a few days ago, *I* didn't even know. Did you know who I was when we met, outside the bank? And how did you find me in the first place?"

Mama Chia gazed out the window for a moment before she answered. "There are other forces at work here — that's the only way I can explain it. I don't often read the local papers, and I almost never read the 'Personals' column. But I was staying at my sister's house on Oahu, for Victor's party, when I found the paper on her coffee table. We were going out, and while I was waiting for her to get ready, I picked up the paper and skimmed through it. When my eyes somehow locked onto your message, a surge of electricity passed through me, I felt a sense of *destiny.*"

I lay very still, but chills ran up and down my spine.

"When I read that ad," she continued, "I could almost see your face, as clearly as I see you now." She tenderly touched my blistered cheeks. "I was so glad you had finally arrived."

"But why would you be glad? Why would you care?"

"When I read the ad, it all came back to me — what Socrates had written about you."

"What did he write?"

"Never mind that now. It's time you ate something," she said. Reaching into her backpack, she pulled out a mango and a papaya.

"I'm not really hungry," I said. "My stomach has shrunk. And I'd rather hear what Socrates wrote about me."

"You've eaten nothing for seven days," she gently chided.

"I've done that before," I replied. "Besides, I needed to loose weight." I pointed to my waist, now much leaner.

"Perhaps — but this fruit has been blessed, and will help you heal more rapidly."

"You really believe that?"

"I don't believe; I *know*," she answered, cutting open a fresh papaya, scooping out the black seeds, and handing me half.

I looked at the fresh fruit. "Maybe I am a little hungry," I said, and nibbled a small piece. Its sweetness melted onto my tongue; I inhaled its aroma. "Good. And it has healing properties?"

"Yes," she said, handing me a slice of ripe mango. "This, too."

Eating obediently, I asked between bites, "So how did you find me — back in Honolulu?"

"Another twist of fate," she replied. "When I found your ad, I decided to somehow make contact — or perhaps observe you for a while, to see if you could find me."

"I never would have found you — you don't even work at a bank."

"Not for six years."

"I guess we found each other," I said, taking another bite of mango.

Mama Chia smiled. "Yes. And now it's time for me to go and for you to rest."

"I'm feeling much better, now — really — and I still want to know why you were so glad I arrived."

She paused before speaking. "There's a bigger picture you don't yet see — one day you may reach out to others...and find the right leverage and make a real difference. Now close your eyes, and sleep."

LEVERAGE, I thought as my eyes closed. The word stuck in my mind, and pulled me back to an incident years before, to a time with Socrates. We were walking back toward the Berkeley campus after a breakfast at Joseph's café. As Soc and I neared campus, a student handed me a flyer. I glanced at it. "Soc," I said, "will you look at this. It's about saving the whales and dolphins. Last week," I sighed, "I got one about oppressed peoples; the week before it was about starving children. Sometimes I feel so guilty, doing all this work on myself when there are so many people in need out there."

Socrates looked at me without expression, but kept walking as if I'd said nothing.

"Did you hear me, Socrates?"

In response, he stopped, turned, and said, "I'll give you five bucks if you can slap me on the cheek."

"What? What does that have to do with — "

"Ten bucks," he interrupted, upping the ante. I figured it was some kind of test, so after a few feints, I took a swing — and found myself on the ground in a painful wrist lock. As Soc helped me up, he said, "Notice how a little leverage can be quite effective?"

"Yeah, I sure did," I replied, shaking my wrist.

"To really help people, you first need to understand them — but first understand yourself, prepare yourself; develop the clarity, the courage, and the sensitivity to exert the right leverage, in the right place, at the right time. Then your actions will have power. History," he added, "holds many examples of individuals and nations who acted without the wisdom to foresee the consequences...."

That was the last thing I remembered before falling into a deep sleep.

THE NEXT MORNING, Sachiko arrived with some fresh fruit and a pitcher of water. Then, with a wave, she said, "Time for school," and ran out the door.

Soon after, Mama Chia entered. She rubbed more of the clean-smelling salve on my face, neck, and chest. "You're healing well — as I expected."

"In a few days, I should be ready to travel." I sat up and stretched, carefully.

"Travel?" she asked. "You think you're ready to go somewhere? And what will you find when you get there — what you found in India?"

"How do you know about India?" I asked.

"When you understand how I know," she said, "you'll be ready to continue your journey." Mama Chia gave me a piercing stare, "Abe Lincoln once said that if he had six hours to chop down a tree, he'd spend the first five hours sharpening the axe. You have a great task ahead, but you are not yet sharpened. It will take time, and require great energy."

"But I'm feeling better all the time. Soon I'll have enough energy."

"It's not your energy I'm talking about," she said with a sigh. "It's mine."

I lay back down, suddenly feeling like a burden. "I really should go," I said. "You have other people to care for; I don't want to impose."

"Impose?" she responded. "Does the diamond impose on the gem polisher? Does the steel impose on the swordsmith? Please, Dan. Stay a while. I can think of no better way to use my energy."

Her words encouraged me. "Well," I said, smiling, "it may not be as hard as you think. I've trained as a gymnast; I know how to work. And I did spend time with Socrates."

"Yes," she said. "Socrates prepared you for me; I'm to prepare you for what follows." She closed the container and put the salve on the bureau.

"What do you have in mind? What do you do around here, anyway? I don't see any banks in the vicinity."

She laughed. "I play different roles, wear different hats for different people. For you, no hat at all." She paused. "Most of the time, I help my friends. Sometimes I just sit and do nothing at all. Sometimes I practice shape-shifting."

"Shape-shifting?"

"Yes."

"What's that?"

"Oh, becoming different things — merging with the spirits of animals, or rocks, or water — that sort of thing. Seeing life from another point of view, if you know what I mean."

"But you don't actually — "

"I need to go now," she said, cutting my question in half. "I have people to see." She picked up her backpack she had set down near the bookcase, grabbed her cane, and walked out the door before I could say another word.

I sat up again with some effort. I could barely see her through the open front door as she limped, swinging her cane, up the winding path into the forest.

I leaned back and watched the narrow rays of sunlight passing through holes in the drawn curtains, and I wondered if I'd ever feel good about the sun again.

I'd suffered a setback, but I had found her. My body tingled with a rising excitement. The road ahead might be difficult — even dangerous — but at least it was open.

CHAPTER 6

Barefoot on a Forest Path

The clearest way into the Universe
is through a forest wilderness.

— John Muir

THE NEXT MORNING found me ravenous, glad for the bowl of fruit on the nightstand. I found a knife and spoon in the drawer and ate two bananas, a passion fruit, and a papaya in quick succession, followed by some macadamia nuts and raw sunflower seeds. I reminded myself to slow down and chew, but the food just seemed to disappear.

Feeling better after breakfast, I decided to explore my surroundings. Swinging my legs over the edge of the bed, I grew dizzy for a few moments, waited for it to pass, then stood. Weak and unsteady, I looked down at myself; I'd lost so much weight, my swim trunks nearly fell off. "I'll have to write a diet book," I muttered. "I'll call it 'The Surfboard Diet' — probably make a million dollars."

Still shaky, I tottered toward a pitcher of water on the dresser, took a slow drink, then made my way to some kind of chemical

toilet in a curtained-off area. It would do just fine. At least my kid-
neys were still functioning.

I stared at my face in an old mirror. With its oozing sores and
scabs, it seemed like the face of a stranger. Parts of my back were
still bandaged. How could that little girl Sachi bear to look at me,
let alone touch me?"

Making my way outside, resting often, I stayed in the shade
of the cabin and trees. The solid ground felt good under me, but
my feet were still tender. Without shoes, I couldn't go far. I wondered if my backpack, with all my belongings, had been discovered. If so, they might think I had drowned. Or, I thought darkly,
maybe a thief had found my wallet, my air tickets, my credit card.
No, I'd hidden the pack too well. It was set in a deep thicket,
covered by dried brush. I'd mention it to Mama Chia the next
time I saw her, which, as it turned out, wasn't to happen for
several more days.

I managed to walk up the trail a little ways until I found a
good vantage point. High above me, in the distance, stood the
bare lava cliffs jutting skyward in the center of the island, above
the thick rain forest. Far below, through the lush trees, I could just
make out bits of blue sky. My cabin, I estimated, lay about halfway
between the upper cliffs and the sea below. Tired, and a little
depressed by my infirmity, I made my way back down the trail to
the cabin, lay down, and slept again.

AS THE DAYS PASSED, my hunger returned in a flood. I ate tropical fruit, then sweet yams, potatoes, corn, taro, and — although
my diet was normally vegetarian — a small sampling of fresh fish
along with some kind of seaweed soup I found on the bureau each
morning, delivered, I suspected, by Sachiko. Mama Chia had
insisted I eat the soup "to help relieve the burns."

Early mornings and late afternoons, I started walking farther, hiking a few hundred yards into the lush valley, up through the rain forest filled with the smooth-skinned kukui tree, the twisting banyan, the towering palm, and the eucalyptus, whose leaves shimmered in the sea breezes. Red and white ginger plants grew everywhere among the delicate *amaumau* ferns, and the red earth was covered with a rich carpet of moss, grasses, and leaves.

Except for the small clearing that surrounded my cabin, everything stood on a slant here. At first I tired quickly, but I soon got my breath back, climbing up into the moist, healing air of the rain forest. Below, a few miles away, sheer cliffs, the *pali,* dropped to the sea. How had they ever carried me up to the cabin?

The next few mornings, traces of dreams lingered in my awareness — images of Mama Chia and the sound of her voice. And each morning I felt unusually refreshed. With amazement, I noticed that my sores had peeled away rapidly, leaving tender new skin, now nearly healed — almost as good as new. My strength was returning and, with it, a renewed sense of urgency. I had found Mama Chia; I was here. Now what? What did I need to learn or do before she would direct me to the next step of my journey?

THE NEXT DAY, the sun was already rising as I awoke, listening to the shrill cries of a bird outside. I rose and set out on another short hike. My bare feet were getting used to the earth.

Later, returning from the hike, I saw Mama Chia entering the cabin, probably expecting to find me in bed. I walked quickly down the grade, nearly slipping on wet leaves, slick from an earlier downpour. Thinking I'd have a little fun with her, and proud of my speedy recovery, I hid behind the shed and peered out as she emerged, puzzled, and looked around. I ducked behind the shed again and put my hand over my mouth to stifle a laugh, then took a deep breath and peeked around the corner again. She was no longer there.

Afraid that she had gone away to look for me, I stepped out from concealment and was about to call her when a hand tapped me on the shoulder; I turned to see her smiling at me. "How did you know where I was?"

"I heard you call to me."

"I didn't call you."

"Yes, you did."

"No, I didn't. I was going to, but — "

"Then how did I know you were here?"

"I asked you that!"

"Then I guess we've come full circle," she said. "Sit down; I brought lunch."

At the word "lunch," I obeyed promptly, sitting on a thick carpet of damp leaves in the shade of a tree. My stomach growled as she offered me sumptuous yams — the best I'd ever tasted — specially prepared rice, and an assortment of crisp vegetables. I don't know how she got it all into her backpack.

The conversation died while we concentrated on eating; finally, between bites, I said, "Thanks. You really know how to cook."

"I didn't make it," she said. "Sachi did."

"Sachiko? Who taught her to cook like that?" I asked.

"Her father."

"She's quite a talent. Her parents must be proud of her."

"They are more than proud of her." Mama Chia put down her food and gazed past the clearing into the thick emerald forest. "Let me tell you a true story: Nine years ago, I helped bring Sachi into the world. When she was four, I also welcomed her little brother.

"Soon after her brother was born, little Sachi began to ask her parents to leave her alone with the new baby. They worried that, like most four-year-olds, she might feel jealous and want to hit or shake him, so they said no. But she showed no signs of jealousy at all; she treated the baby with kindness — and her pleas to be left alone with him became more urgent. They decided to allow it.

"Elated, she went into the baby's room and shut the door, but it opened a crack — enough for her curious parents to peek in and listen. They saw little Sachi walk quietly up to her baby brother, put her face close to his, and say quietly, 'Baby, tell me what God feels like. I'm starting to forget.'"

"She said that?" I asked, in awe.

"Yes."

After a long pause, I remarked, "I can understand why she's your apprentice."

We sat in silence a while, in the shade of a tree, until Mama Chia said, "Tomorrow we go for a hike."

"Together?" I asked.

"No," she teased. "You'll take the high road, and I'll take the low road."

I still didn't know Mama Chia very well, and it was sometimes hard to tell whether she was joking. Seeing my confusion, Mama Chia laughed, and said, "Yes, we'll hike together."

I had a feeling things were about to pick up. Then I looked down at my worn trunks, and bare feet and chest. I looked up at her and explained, "I don't know if I can hike far without — "

Smiling, she pointed behind me. "Look behind the tree."

"My backpack!" I cried, amazed. As she grinned, I ran over to it and looked inside. My wallet — with a few dollars cash and credit card — my watch, a clean pair of shorts, my sneakers, toothbrush, and razor — everything was there.

"Sachi's father was working on a carpentry job on Oahu," she explained. "I sent him to Makapuu Point to find your things. He said you'd hidden them well."

"When can I meet him and thank him?" I asked.

"He's looking forward to meeting you, too, but he had to go back to Oahu to finish the job; he'll return in a few weeks. I'm glad you have new shorts," she added, holding her nose with one hand and pointing to my ragged trunks with the other, "so you can wash those."

Smiling, I took her hand. "Thank you, Mama Chia. I'm really grateful for all you've done."

"Yes, I've certainly done a lot," she said, brushing off my thanks with a wave of her hand. "Have you heard about the new breed of dog that's a cross between a pit bull and a collie? First it takes your arm off, then it runs for help." She smiled. "I've already done enough damage; this is my way of 'running for help.'"

Packing the remains of our lunch, she stood. I started to stand, too, but I was so weak I could barely get up. "I feel like such a wimp." I said as she walked me back into the cabin.

"Your muscles only feel weak because your body is using the energy to heal the rest of you. You've been through a great deal; most people would have given up and died. Your Basic Self is very strong."

"My basic what?" I asked, puzzled, as I sat down on the bed.

"Your Basic Self," Mama Chia replied. "A part of who you are — an awareness separate from your conscious mind. Didn't Socrates teach you about the three selves?"

"No," I replied, intrigued. "But it sounds like an interesting concept."

Mama Chia stood, walked to the window, and gazed outside. "The three selves are much more than a concept, Dan; they are as real to me as the earth, the trees, the sky, and the sea."

Mama Chia sat against the windowsill and said, "A few hundred years ago, before the invention of the microscope, almost no one believed in the existence of bacteria and viruses, and so, humanity remained powerless before these unseen invaders. Those who did believe in their existence were labeled 'crackpots.'

"I, too, work with elements invisible to most people — with nature spirits and subtle energies. But 'invisible' is not the same as imaginary, Dan. Each new generation forgets this, and so the cycle repeats itself — the blind leading the blind," she said without a trace of rancor. "Ignorance, as well as wisdom, is handed down from one generation to the next like a precious heirloom.

"The three selves — the Basic Self, Conscious Self, and Higher Self — are part of a secret teaching. The secrets have never been hidden, really, but few people are interested, and fewer still have the eyes to see."

She paced, in her limping style, across the room to the doorway, and turned back toward me. "When I speak to you of 'invisible things,' know that *they are not invisible to me.* But what is true for me does not have to be true for you; I'm not telling you what to believe — only sharing my experience." She poured a glass of water and handed it to me. "When you're strong enough — if Socrates has prepared you well — I'll be able to take you to the edge, and point the way; all you'll have to do is open your eyes and leap." She walked to the door and said, "Now rest."

"Wait," I said, sitting up. "Before you go, can you tell me a little more about the three selves? I'd like to hear more — "

"And there's more I'd like to tell you," she interrupted. "But first you need to sleep."

"I am tired," I said, yawning.

"Yes. Tomorrow we'll walk, and tomorrow we'll talk." Through the open doorway, I watched her swinging her cane and limping back into the forest. I yawned again, then my eyes shut and the world went black.

BOOK TWO

Illuminations

The real voyage of discovery consists

not in seeking new landscapes,

but in having new eyes.

— Marcel Proust

CHAPTER 7

The Three Selves

You cannot transcend what you do not know.
To go beyond yourself, you must know yourself.

— Sri Nisargadatta Maharaj

THE NEXT DAY, THE BIRDS' SONG seemed sweeter and the world more beautiful. My strength was returning; only a few scabs remained. Running my hand across my two-week growth of beard, I decided I would keep it for now.

After filling up on tropical fruit and home-baked bread that had mysteriously appeared on my chest of drawers — another gift from Sachi, I guessed — I stepped outside, stripped naked, and showered in a warm, drenching downpour. The rain passed as quickly as it had come, leaving clear, sunny skies.

I had just finished combing my wet hair and smoothing on a thick layer of sunscreen when Mama Chia came limping down the path with her familiar backpack, cane, and a large muumuu dress — her typical hiking outfit, I learned.

After a brief greeting, she led me down a narrow, winding path toward the sea. As she lumbered along the slippery trail, a few feet ahead of me, I could see it wasn't easy for her to get around and was struck by her determination.

She stopped a few times — once, to point out a colorful bird, another time to show me a small waterfall and pond, hidden from the casual eye. After we sat a while, listening to the sounds of water falling into a pond, I offered to carry her backpack for her, but she refused, saying, "Maybe next time."

Conversation was sparse after that. We both had to concentrate on our footing along the perennially muddy trail, crisscrossed by tree roots.

Finally, we made our way down a steep ravine and emerged into a small sandy clearing, one of the few beach areas among the rocky cliffs. On either side of us, lava rock shot straight up into the sky to form the towering cliffs.

Mama Chia took a light blanket out of her pack and spread it on the beach. The tide had just gone out, leaving the sand smooth, hard, and wet. The relaxing sea breeze felt good on my face and chest.

"Mama Chia," I asked, "maybe it's my imagination, but I've only been here about ten days — is that right?"

"Yes."

"And didn't I nearly die of exposure and thirst?"

"Yes," she answered again.

"Well, aren't I healing awfully fast?"

She nodded. "I've been working with you at night."

"What do you mean?"

"When you sleep, your Conscious Self steps back; that's when I can work directly with the Basic Self — your subconscious — which is in charge of healing your body."

"You were going to tell me more about this 'Basic Self.'"

Mama Chia stared at me, as if considering something. Then

she picked up a nearby twig and drew a circle in the sand. "Better
to show than tell," she said, scratching the figure of a human body
within the circle, his arms outstretched — a crude rendition of
Leonardo da Vinci's famous drawing.

Without further comment, she sat down on a mound of sand,
crossed her legs, and said, "I need to do some inner work to
recharge my batteries. Unless you've learned to do the same, I suggest you take a nap. Perhaps later we can talk."

"But — "

With one breath, Mama Chia seemed instantly to go into a
deep trance. I watched her for a few moments, then my attention
turned once again to her drawing in the sand. Feeling suddenly
drowsy on this sultry day, glad for the shade of the sheltering cliffs,
I stretched out on the blanket and closed my eyes.

My thoughts turned to my wife and daughter, back in Ohio
— light-years away, it seemed, from this hidden cove, where I
rested a few feet away from a woman shaman whose full powers
were yet to be revealed, and whose existence had been unknown
to me a few weeks before. And I had found her, against all odds,
against all hope.

Life is amazing, I thought. And the next moment, I fell head-
long into a dreamlike vision.

I WAS ASLEEP, YET WIDE AWAKE. Mama Chia's smiling face flashed
before me, then vanished. In the blackness that followed, a human
form appeared: a man's body within a circle, his arms outstretched
— not the figure Mama Chia had sketched in the sand, but a vivid
image of da Vinci's original.

Then, in the blink of an eye, I saw my own body appear
within the circle, and it started spinning, cartwheeling through
space.

From my point of awareness, I saw my physical form come to rest, standing upright in a forest, under a starry sky. Illuminated by the pale moon, clothed only in a pair of shorts, the figure stood with arms open wide, as if to embrace life itself, with head tilting slightly up and to the left, gazing up through the trees at the stars sparkling in the black velvet sky. I could see all this in the sharpest detail — every moon shadow on every leaf.

Then, three glowing lights appeared within and around the body, separate and distinct from the body's auras or energy fields. First, my attention rested on an earthly reddish glow illuminating the belly region. I recognized this instantly as the Basic Self.

My attention shifted to the head, where the white light of awareness filled the Conscious Self, shining so brightly that the head disappeared.

Then my awareness rose above the head, where I began to see a swirl of radiant, iridescent colors....

Suddenly, everything tilted crazily, and thunder exploded in the distance. Flashes of lightning ripped the sky. The wind wailed, and trees came crashing down. Then the physical form in front of me split into three separate beings.

The Higher Self, which I had only begun to see in the blaze of radiant color, vanished. The two beings that remained changed into distinct physical forms. The Basic Self now appeared as a child, surrounded by a reddish glow. It quailed and shrank back as the next flash of lightning lit its face, revealing primal fear.

The Conscious Self took the form of a gray robot, whose computerized head glowed with electricity; it whirred and clicked, then looked up stiffly at the sky, expressionless, as if sorting information and weighing the best course of action.

With the next crack of thunder, the child bolted, and ran instinctively for the cover of a hollow tree. I found myself following it, and watched as it huddled there. The child seemed shy, and didn't speak. As I gazed at it, I felt myself drawn deeper into its glow.

In a microsecond, my consciousness had merged with that of the child. I saw life through its eyes, and experienced all its emotions. Confused by myriad images of past storms and associations going back lifetimes, I huddled instinctively as fearful pictures — a patchwork of genetic memories — flashed through my childlike awareness. What I lacked in clear logic, I improvised with primal instinct. I felt a vast storehouse of vital energy; my emotions were wide open, amplified. Motivated by a primitive impulse to survive, to seek pleasure and avoid pain, I felt more inclined to act than contemplate. My inner world was untamed, unrefined by culture, rules, or logic. In my wildness and fleshiness, I was energy in motion — closely tied to the natural world, completely at home in the body, with its feelings and impulses.

I had little means to perceive refined beauty or higher faith; I knew only good feelings and bad feelings. Right now, I felt a compelling need for guidance, for someone to interpret for me, to reassure and direct me. I needed the Conscious Self.

Just then, having devised its plan, the robot-computer also entered the hollow tree. But it ignored me, the child, almost completely, as if I didn't matter. Resentful and feeling unappreciated, I nudged it to get its attention. Why didn't it listen to me? After all, I'd found shelter first. It still ignored me; I pushed it and slapped it, with no better results. Furious, I ran outside, got a rock, and smashed it into the robot's leg. That got its attention.

"What — do — you — want?" it asked in a monotone.

"Listen to me!" I cried.

In the next instant, my consciousness left the child and merged with the robot-computer. I looked through the eyes of this reasoning machine, and saw the world with objectivity and icy calm. The child I had been now appeared as a distraction. I formulated a solution to appease it.

Just then, the storm passed, and the child ran outside to play. I set this problem aside and walked stiffly into the forest. Untroubled by emotions or sentiment, my world was orderly, structured, and terribly limited. I saw the forest in shades of gray. Beauty to me was a definition, a category. I knew nothing of the Higher Self, or faith. I sought what was useful and constructive. The body to me was a necessary burden, a machine that enabled me to move and reproduce — a tool of the mind.

Safe within the computer mind, I was immune to the vagaries of emotion. And yet, without the playful spirit, the emotional energy, and the vitality of the child, I didn't really live; I only existed in a sterile world of problems and solutions.

My awareness awoke, as if from a dream, and feeling a sudden and overwhelming urge to feel the forest once again, to experience the rising energies of life, I broke free of the Conscious Self.

From my new vantage point, I saw both the Conscious Self and the Basic Self with their backs to each other, in their own worlds. If only they were together, how much richer both their lives would be.

I appreciated the childlike innocence and instinctive body wisdom of the Basic Self; I valued the reason, logic, and learning abilities of the robot-computer, the Conscious Self. But without the inspiration of the Higher Self, life felt insipid, shallow, and incomplete.

As I realized this, I heard the Higher Self calling me from somewhere in the forest, and I felt an intense longing to merge with it. I recognized this longing as one I had felt for many years, perhaps my whole life. For the first time, I knew what I had been searching for.

Moments later, I was captured by the Conscious Self again. Trapped within its steel mind, I heard its droning voice, slow at first, then more rapidly playing again and again: "I — am — all — there — is. The — Higher — Self — is — an — illusion."

My awareness snapped back into the childlike Basic Self once again. Now all I wanted to do was play, and feel good, and powerful, and secure.

Again, I snapped back into the Conscious Self and saw one reality — then rebounded back into the Basic Self and felt another. Faster and faster, I bounced back and forth between Conscious Self and Basic Self, mind and body, robot and child, thinking and feeling, logic and impulse. Faster and faster.

I SAT UP, STARING INTO SPACE — terrified, sweating, crying out softly. Then, gradually, I became aware of my surroundings: the sheltered ocean cove, the warm beach, a sky turning pink and purple above a calm sea. And nearby sat Mama Chia, unmoving, gazing at me.

Shaking off the remnants of this vision, I tried to slow my breathing and relax. I managed to explain, "I — I had a bad dream."

She spoke slowly and deliberately: "Was it a bad dream, or a mirror of your life?"

"I don't know what you mean," I said. But I was lying; I knew this as soon as the words were out of my mouth. With my new-found awareness of the three selves, I could no longer maintain the pretense of being "together." I was a self divided, wavering between the self-centered, childlike needs of the Basic Self, and the cold detachment of the Conscious Self — out of touch with my Higher Self.

These past years, my mind had constantly smothered my

feelings; it had ignored and devalued them. Rather than acknowledge the pain and passion I felt, my Conscious Self had maintained control and swept my feelings, and my relationships, under the rug.

I now understood that the physical symptoms I had experienced back home — the infections, the aches, and the pains — had been my Basic Self, crying for attention like a young child; it wanted me to express all the feelings inside. Suddenly I understood the aphorism "The organs weep the tears the eyes refuse to shed." And something Wilhelm Reich had once said came into my mind: "Unexpressed emotion is stored in the muscles of the body." These troubling revelations depressed and disheartened me. I saw how far I still had to go.

"Are you all right?" Mama Chia asked.

"Sure, I'm okay," I started to answer, then stopped myself. "No, I don't feel all right. I feel drained and depressed."

"Good," she said, beaming. "You've learned something. Now you're back on the right track."

Nodding, I asked, "In the dream, I only experienced two of the selves. My Higher Self vanished. Why did it leave me?"

"It didn't leave you, Dan — it was there all the time — but you were so preoccupied with your Basic Self and your Conscious Self that you couldn't see it, or feel its love and support."

"Well, how *can* I feel it? Where do I go from here?"

"A good question — a very good question," she said, laughing to herself as she stood. Then she slipped her pack over her shoulders, and started slowly up the rocky trail. Still full of unanswered questions, I followed.

The sand turned to stones and earth as we climbed up a steep path along the cliff face. I turned and looked back at the cove, slightly below us. The tide was coming in. Twenty yards away, a wave rushed up close to the figure Mama Chia had drawn in the sand. I blinked and looked again. Where the figure and circle had been, I thought I saw three figures — a small body, like that of a child; a square, boxlike figure; and a large oval — just before a wave rushed past, washing the sand clean.

The climb up was more difficult than the hike down. Mama Chia seemed in high spirits, but my mood was glum. Neither of us spoke. An array of images from the vision passed through my mind as I followed her up the path into the darkening forest.

By the time we entered the clearing, the half-moon had neared its zenith. Mama Chia bade me good night and continued up the path.

I stood outside the cabin for a few moments, listening to the crickets' song. The warm night breeze seemed to pass right through me. I didn't realize how fatigued I felt until I entered the cabin. I vaguely remember visiting the bathroom, then falling onto the bed. I heard the crickets a moment more, then silence. That night, in a dream, I searched for my Higher Self, but found only emptiness.

— CHAPTER 8 —

Eyes of the Shaman

A great teacher never strives to explain her vision;
she simply invites you to stand beside her and see for yourself.

— The Rev. R. Inman

NOT YET FULLY AWAKE — in more ways than one, I concluded —
I opened my eyes and saw Mama Chia standing by my bedside. At
first I thought I was still dreaming, but I came back to earth
quickly when she yelled, "Out of bed!" I jumped up so fast I
nearly fell over.

"I'll — I'll be ready in a minute," I slurred, still groggy,
vowing to get up before she arrived next time. I stumbled into
the bathroom, slipped into my shorts, and stepped outside into a
rainsquall for my morning shower.

Dripping wet, I stepped back inside and grabbed a towel. "It
must be nearly noon."

"Just after eleven," she said.

"Whoa, I — "

"On Thursday," she interrupted, "you've been out cold for thirty-six hours."

I nearly dropped the towel. "Almost *two days?*" I sat down heavily on the bed.

"You look upset. Did you miss an appointment?" she asked.

"No, I guess not." I looked up at her. "Did I?"

"Not with me, you didn't; besides, appointments are not native to Hawaii." She explained, "Mainlanders tried to import them, but it's like trying to sell beef to vegetarians. You feeling better?"

"Much better," I answered, toweling off my hair. "But I'm not exactly sure what I'm supposed to be *doing* here or what you're supposed to help me with. Are you going to help me see my Higher Self?"

"That remains to be seen," she answered, smiling at her play on words, and handing me my shirt.

"Mama Chia," I said, putting on the shirt, "those things I saw — that vision on the beach — did you hypnotize me?"

"Not exactly. What you saw came from the Inner Records."

"What are they?"

"That's not easy to describe. You can call it the 'universal unconscious,' or the 'journal of Spirit.' Everything is written there."

"Everything?"

"Yes," she replied. "Everything."

"Can you... read these records?"

"Sometimes — it depends."

"Well, how did *I* read them?"

"Let's just say I turned the pages for you."

"Like a mother reading to her child?"

"Something like that."

rain stopped, so she stepped outside. I followed her to a log near the shed and sat down. "Mama Chia," I said, "I need to talk with you about something that's really starting to bother me. It seems like the more I learn, the worse it gets. You see — "

She interrupted me. "Just handle what's in front of you now, and the future will take care of itself. Otherwise, you'll spend most of your life wondering which foot you'll use to step off the curb when you're still only halfway to the corner."

"What about planning ahead, and preparing for the future?"

"Plans are useful, but don't get attached to them; life has too many surprises. Preparation, on the other hand, has value, even if the future you planned never comes."

"How's that?"

She paused before answering. "An old friend of mine here on the island, Sei Fujimoto — you haven't met him yet — has worked as a gardener and handyman most of his life. But photography was his first love. I never saw a man so passionate about images on paper. Years ago, he would spend most of his days searching for the perfect shot. Fuji especially loved landscapes: the shapes of trees, waves breaking with the sun shining through them, and clouds by the light of the moon, or the morning sun. When he wasn't taking pictures, he was developing them in his own darkroom at home.

"Fuji practiced photography for nearly thirty years, accumulating in that time a treasury of inspired photographs. He kept the negatives in a locked file in his office. He sold some photos, and gave others to friends.

"Then, about six years ago, a fire destroyed all the photographs he had taken over those thirty years, and all the negatives, as well as most of his equipment. He had no fire insurance — all the evidence and fruits of a generation of creative work — a total and irreplaceable loss.

"Fuji mourned this as he might mourn the loss of a child. Three years before, he *had* lost a child, and he understood very well that suffering was a relative thing, and that if he could make it through his child's death, he could make it through anything.

"But more than that, he understood the bigger picture, and came to a growing realization that something of great value remained that was never touched by the fire: *Fuji had learned to see life in a different way.* Every day, when he got up, he saw a world of light and shadow, shapes and textures — a world of beauty and harmony and balance.

"When he shared this insight with me, Dan, he was so happy! His realization mirrors that of the Zen masters who share with their students that all paths, all activities — professions, sports, arts, crafts — serve as a means of internal development, merely a boat to get across the river. Once you get across, you no longer need the boat." Mama Chia took a deep breath and smiled serenely at me.

"I'd like to meet Sei Fujimoto."

"And you will," she assured me.

"I just remembered something Socrates once told me: 'It's not the way *to* the peaceful warrior; it's the way *of* the peaceful warrior. *The journey itself creates the warrior.*'"

"Socrates always had a way with words," she said. Then she sighed wistfully. "You know...he and I were once lovers."

"What? When? How? What happened?"

"Everything...and nothing happened," she said. "We were together for a time. I believe it was healing for him, after...we won't speak of that — you'll have to ask him. In any case, he was called elsewhere. And so was I. So we never — well, that was a long time ago. Years later, I married my late husband, Bradford Johnson. He was a special man, too — but more conventional — not like Socrates...."

"Will you tell me more," I said, "about when you met Socrates, and about his life? What was his real name? Surely not everyone called him 'Socrates.'"

A wistful smile appeared on Mama Chia's face. "I may tell a few stories about my life some other time. But it's for... Socrates to share the rest. I expect that he'll let you know in his own way, in his own time. But right now, I have other business, and you need more time to consider what you've learned, before — " she stopped herself. "Before what will come."

"I'm ready anytime."

Mama Chia stared at me a moment but said nothing. She reached into her pack and tossed me a small package of macadamia nuts. "See you tomorrow." With that, she left.

I DID FEEL STRONGER, but despite my bravado, I wasn't really ready for anything rigorous. I spent the rest of the morning in a restful reverie — sitting and gazing at the trees surrounding my home here on Molokai. A troubling feeling was growing inside me, but I didn't have words for it yet. Preoccupied, I hardly tasted the small chunks of bread, the macadamia nuts, or the fruit I consumed.

As the afternoon sun touched the tips of the trees at the edge of the clearing, I realized I was lonely. Strange, I reflected, I used to like being alone. I had chosen solitude for most of my college years. But after floating out on that surfboard — when I thought I might never see another human being again — something changed. And now —

My thoughts were interrupted by a bright "Hi!" off to my left. Sachi hopped, skipped, and danced toward me. Her jet black hair,

cut short like Mama Chia's, bounced and swirled with each movement. Jumping from a stone to a log, she skipped over and set down
a small package. "I brought some more bread — made it myself."

"Thank you, Sachi. That was very thoughtful."

"No, it wasn't," she replied. "I didn't think much at all.
How're you feeling?"

"Much better, now that you've dropped in. I've been alone so
much I was starting to talk to myself."

"I do that sometimes," she said.

"Well, then, now that you're here, we can sit and both talk to
ourselves — no, wait," I teased. "I have an idea: Why don't we sit
here and talk to each other?"

She smiled at my corny attempt at humor. "Sounds okay.
Want to see the frog pond?"

"Sure."

"It's not far. Follow me," she said, scampering into the forest.

Doing my best to keep up, I saw her up ahead, appearing and
disappearing about ten yards away, dodging around trees. By the
time I caught up with her, she was sitting on a large rock, pointing to a couple of frogs. One graced us with a loud croak.

"You weren't kidding, girl; these are some great frogs."

"That's the queen over there," she said. "And I call this one
here 'Grumpy' because he always hops away when I pet him."
Sachi reached slowly down and stroked one of the frogs. "My
brother likes to feed 'em, but I don't like squishy bugs — used to,
but not anymore." Then, like a little woods sprite, she bounded
off, back toward the cabin. I said a silent good-bye to Grumpy,
and walked after her. As I left, I heard a loud "Grrrumph." I
turned to see the water splash as the frog dove under.

Back in the clearing, Sachi was practicing some dance steps.
"Mama Chia showed me this," she said. "She teaches me a lot of
things."

"I bet she does," I replied. Then I had an idea. "Maybe I could teach you something, too. Can you do a cartwheel?"

"Sort of," she replied, throwing her arms down and legs up. "I bet I look like one of those frogs," she giggled. "Can you show me one?"

"I guess so — I used to be pretty good at it," I said, doing a one-arm cartwheel over the log.

"Wow!" she said, impressed. "That was smooth." Inspired, she tried again, improving slightly.

"Here, Sachi, let me show you again," I said.

The rest of the afternoon passed quickly. And Sachi learned a graceful cartwheel.

I spotted a bright red flower growing nearby, and on impulse I picked it and placed it in her hair. "You know, I have a daughter named Holly — younger than you — I miss her. I'm glad you came by to visit."

"Me, too," she replied. Touching the flower, Sachi graced me with the sweetest smile. "Well, I gotta go. Thanks for showing me a cartwheel." She ran up the trail, then turned and called back to me, "Don't forget your bread!"

Her smile made my day.

When Mama Chia arrived the next morning, I was ready and waiting, tossing pebbles at a tree. "Want some fresh bread?" I said. "I already ate, but if you're hungry — "

"I'm fine," she said. "Let's get moving. We have miles to cover by sundown."

"Where are we going?" I asked as we left the cabin and headed up the path.

"That way." She pointed up to the central range of ridges formed of black lava rock, several thousand feet above us. Handing me her backpack, she said, simply, "You're strong enough now to carry this."

We hiked slowly upward along an ever-steepening trail, with many turns and switchbacks. Mama Chia walked steadily upward. The forest was silent, except for the cry of an occasional bird, and my rhythmic tread, beating a countertempo to her swinging cane and limping gait.

She stopped every now and then to admire a colorful bird or to point out an unusual tree or small waterfall.

By late morning, my concerns began rising to the surface, and I called to her. "Mama Chia, Socrates once told me I haven't really learned something until I could do it."

She stopped, turned to me, and nodded, saying, "There's a proverb: 'I hear and I forget, I see and I remember, I do and I understand.'"

"That's just it," I confessed. "I've heard about and seen a lot of things, but I haven't really *done* anything. I've learned a little about healing, but can I heal? I know about the Higher Self, but I can't feel it."

My words finally spilled out in sudden frustration. "I was a world champion gymnast; I graduated from the University of California; I have a beautiful daughter. I take care of myself, eat right, do the right thing. I'm a *college professor* for God's sake — so why do I feel like I've done nothing? I have this sense that there's something else I'm supposed to be doing. It drives me crazy. And even after my training with Socrates, my life feels like it's falling apart. I used to believe that if I learned enough, if I made all the right moves, that life was going to get easier, more under control, but now it only feels worse — like something slipping away and I don't know how to stop it. It's like I got lost along the way. I know there are people a lot worse off than I am. I'm not being victimized by anyone; I'm not living in poverty or hunger or oppression. I guess it sounds like I'm whining or complaining, but I'm not feeling sorry for myself — I just want it to stop."

I looked into her eyes and told her, "I once broke my leg pretty badly — my thigh bone was shattered in about forty pieces — so I know what pain feels like. And this feels just as real to me. Do you understand?"

She nodded in a way that showed she understood. "Pain and suffering are a part of everyone's life. They just take different forms."

"Do you believe you can help me find whatever it is I'm looking for?" I asked, an edge of desperation in my voice.

"If I didn't believe I could help, we wouldn't be here," she answered before turning and continuing her steady, limping gait up the trail.

AS WE ROSE UP OUT OF THE FOREST, the trees thinned out; the moss and leaves beneath our feet gave way to reddish brown earth, which turned to mud as a torrential rain came and passed quickly. I slipped now and then. Mama Chia, though slow paced, was sure-footed. Finally, just when I thought she had forgotten my plea, she spoke.

"Dan, have you ever considered that no *one* person could ever create a building? No matter how smart, how strong, a single individual may be, he can't make a building without the combined efforts of architects, contractors, laborers, accountants, manufacturers, truckers, chemists, and hundreds more. No one is smarter than all of us."

"But what does that have to do with — "

"For example, take Socrates," she continued. "He possesses many talents, but he understood that he could not force-feed your psyche. He could only teach you what you had ears to hear or eyes to see.

"When Socrates wrote to me, he predicted to me that you'd be hard on yourself — that you got excitable — and that now and then I might have to calm you down." She turned back, smiling, before she continued her slow climb. "He also told of the seeds he had sown within your mind and heart. I'm here to nourish them — to help them quicken and grow.

"Socrates helped you clear away some of your deepest illusions. He could not awaken you — you weren't yet ready — but he did make you aware that you were sleeping, and revealed to you an array of possibilities, a preview of coming attractions. He established a foundation so that now, even if you can't always hear, you're at least willing to listen. If he hadn't done his work well, you would never have found me."

"But I didn't find you. You found me."

"No matter how strange the circumstances of our meeting, I don't believe it would have happened had you not been ready. That's how these things work. I might not have chosen to work with you; you might not have come to the party. Who can say?"

We stopped briefly to survey the view as we entered the highlands, not far from the base of the rocky peak. Green treetops stretched almost as far as I could see. The moist, humid air dampened my arms and forehead. As I wiped the moisture from my brow, Mama Chia put her arm on my shoulder and said, "In any event, here we are — and we're all in training together. I can help you turn your experience into lessons, and your lessons into wisdom. For now, I can only encourage you to trust the process of your life, and to remember the law of faith...."

"Like believing in God?" I asked.

"Faith has little to do with belief," she answered. "Faith is the courage to live your life as if everything that happens does so for your highest good and learning. Like it or not."

She stopped, and knelt down next to a yellow flower, growing up through a small crack in a large stone. "Our lives are like this flower. We appear so fragile, and yet, when we meet obstacles, we push through them, always growing toward the Light."

I touched the yellow petals. "But flowers grow slowly. I don't feel I have that much time. I feel like I should do something now, like it can't wait any longer."

"Flowers grow in their own good time. It's not easy, seeing the path twist and disappear ahead, knowing it's a long climb. You want to act because that's what you have been trained to do. But first understand."

"Understanding without acting does nothing," I said.

"Yet acting without understanding may create even more problems. Sometimes you need to simply relax into life, and to trust." She took a deep breath. "No matter how pressing life may feel at times, Dan, there's no need to rush, and nowhere to rush to. You have plenty of time to accomplish what you wish."

"This life?"

"Or the next."

"I'd like to start a little sooner than that," I said. "I have an ache inside — maybe it's a message from my Basic Self — and it's prodding me to get on with it. Whatever 'it' is."

Mama Chia stopped again and looked at me. "In the darkest, most chaotic times — when things fall apart — such times often mark quickening as your mind readies itself to make a leap. When you feel like you're going nowhere, stagnating, even slipping back-ward — your soul is only backing up to get a running start."

"You really believe this?"

"What I believe isn't the point. You have to go beyond belief to direct experience. Consider it for yourself. Look at your life deeply, right now. Ask your inner knower; your Basic Self knows

— it has already told me that you're about to make the leap — maybe not today, or tomorrow, but soon enough. And just as Socrates prepared you for me, I'll do my part to get you ready for the next step."

"You make it sound simple."

"It is simple; just not easy. But it could be far easier if you weren't still stuck in your drama, so serious. You're like a gnat on a TV screen, Dan — all you see is a bunch of dots. Open your eyes! There is a bigger picture. Each of us has our role to play. You are playing your part to perfection. And when the time is right, you'll not only find your purpose; you'll realize you never lost it. You're searching for your path in life even as you walk upon it. For now, fully embrace all three selves. Let them work together in harmony and cooperation, your head in the clouds and your feet on the ground."

Gazing ahead, she added, "We certainly have work to do together, you and I. We're going to prepare you the same way we're climbing this mountain — one step at a time." At that, she turned and continued upward. I felt encouraged by her words, but my body, feeling the exertion, was growing weary. Yet Mama Chia somehow limped on and on.

"Where exactly are we going, anyway?" I asked, panting.

"To the top."

"And what are we going to do when we get there?"

"You'll find that out when we arrive," she said, heading up the rocky trail.

The hike soon became steeper, like an endless stairway. The air grew thinner and our breathing more labored with each step as we climbed toward the peak of Kamakau, almost five thousand feet high.

TWO HOURS LATER, just before dusk, we reached the peak and stepped at last onto level ground. With a wave of her hand, Mama Chia directed my eyes to an incredible panorama of the island of Molokai. Turning slowly around, I gazed out over the expanse of lush green forest at the sea. The edge of the sky was ablaze with color as the setting sun painted the clouds red, purple, orange, and pink.

"Well, here we are," I said with a sigh.

"Yes, here we are," she echoed, still gazing at the setting sun.

"Now that we're here, what are we going to do?"

"Gather some wood. We'll camp nearby tonight. I know a spot. Tomorrow, we reach our destination." She pointed toward the eastern tip of the island.

She led me to a small waterfall, where we drank deeply of the sparkling water, rich with minerals. Nearby stood a rock overhang that would shelter us in case of sudden rain. Glad to rest my wobbling legs, I swung Mama Chia's pack off my shoulders. I had no idea how this elderly woman, smaller than I but heavier, limping along mile after mile of rugged terrain, could sustain this kind of effort.

We made a fire big enough to heat some rocks and bury them with foil-wrapped yams. Served with some raw vegetables, the yams tasted as delectable as any meal I'd ever eaten.

We made our beds of a thick moss, and put some small branches in the fire — not for warmth, but for the glow, and the comforting crackle.

As we settled in for the night and lay gazing up through the palm fronds into endless space, I said, "Ever since I was floating out there — on the surfboard — I've been thinking a lot about death. A few nights ago, the face of an old friend appeared to me. He was a student at Oberlin, so young and full of life. Then he was diagnosed with a terminal illness. He told me that he prayed a lot. But he died just the same."

"Our prayers are always answered," said Mama Chia. "But sometimes God says no."

"Why would God say no?"

"Why does a loving parent say no? Sometimes children's wants run counter to their needs. People turn to God when their foundations are shaking, only to discover it is God who's shaking them. The conscious mind cannot always foresee what is for the highest good."

"Easy for you to say — "

"Not so easy, but this is how I live...." She was silent for a time, but then I heard her voice again: "As a young girl...when I first met the man you call Socrates — my body was slim and supple and full of life. Now I have physical challenges — painful at times, but every challenge has brought hidden gifts, though I didn't always appreciate them at the time. One gift is deeper compassion. For someone else, the gift might be greater sensitivity to the body, or a stronger motivation to take better care of oneself, or to relax and play more."

"Discomfort is one way our Basic Self gets our attention."

"It sure works for me," I said, gazing into the fire.

"Yes, but I don't recommend it as a habit," she added. "Although pain may serve as a wake-up call, it's usually the Basic Self's second-to-last resort. It only sends harsh messages when the gentler ones — your intuitions and dreams — have been ignored."

"What's the Basic Self's last resort?"

"Death," she said. "And it happens, in one form or the other, to many who were unable or unwilling to listen. Basic Selves, like children, are loyal and not easily alienated. They may receive a lot of abuse. But when they've had enough..."

She didn't need to finish her sentence. In the silence, I asked, "If the Basic Self is in charge of the body, it can cause or cure any disease, right?"

"Under the right circumstances, if it's permitted within the destiny of that individual, yes."

"Then medicines don't really matter."

"Medicines are one way to assist the Basic Self — they're a gift from the natural world," she said, reaching up and plucking a seedpod from a nearby bush. Opening the pod, she showed me the small seeds, and said, "Basic Selves, as you've experienced, have a close connection to the natural world; each plant and herb carries specific messages and energies that the Basic Self understands. So does each color, or aroma, or sound. Or dance, for that matter.

"Healing is a great mystery, even for today's physicians; we are still discovering nature's laws of balance. But as we get in closer touch with our Basic Selves and the subtle forces at work, we will see more 'miracles.'"

"Most physicians tend to rely on their Conscious Selves, on their minds rather than on their intuitions, don't they?"

"It's not a matter of trusting the Basic Self or the Conscious Self," she replied. "It's a matter of trusting *both* — each at the appropriate time. The Arabs have a saying: 'Trust in God, but tie your camel.' It's important to trust the Basic Self to heal a cut, for example, but the Conscious Self reminds us to use a bandage.

"If you overeat junk food, smoke cigarettes, drink too much alcohol, or use other drugs — if you exhaust yourself, or hold in your emotions — you make it harder for the Basic Self to do its job and maintain a strong immune system; it can't always heal without the cooperation of the Conscious Self; it can only send painful body messages to get your attention. Prayer alone may not be enough; also do what you can to assist. Francis Cardinal Spellman once said, 'Pray as if everything depended on God, and work as if everything depended on man.'"

I watched Mama Chia with growing admiration and wonder. "Mama Chia, how do you know so much? Where did you learn all these things?"

She said nothing at first. I glanced over at her in the firelight, thinking she had fallen asleep. But her eyes were wide open, as if staring into another world. Finally, she answered, "I'll think on it tonight. Perhaps I'll tell you some of my story tomorrow. We still have a long hike ahead." With that, she turned on her side and went quickly to sleep. I lay awake a while before joining her, staring at the dying embers of the fire.

CHAPTER 9

A Well-Rounded Woman

God comforts the disturbed
and disturbs the comfortable.

— Unknown

IN THE MORNING, a refreshing shower under the waterfall helped clear the stiffness from my legs, back, and shoulders. Though I hadn't regained my full strength, the simple diet and outdoor exercise brought renewed vitality.

After a small breakfast of papaya, banana, and water from the falls, we continued along the range of volcanic rock that burst from the sea a million years before, breathing to the rhythm of our footsteps. Mama Chia must have known this range intimately; she seemed instinctively to know the correct path at every turn.

As we walked, I once again asked her to tell me about her life.

"I don't usually talk much about my life," she began. "But I feel it's important for you to know a little."

"Why is that?"

"I'm not certain, but I trust my instincts."

"Well, you have my attention," I said, walking closely behind her on the narrowing trail.

She began: "I was born here, on Molokai, in 1882. My father was part Hawaiian and part Japanese, the same as my mother. Like this island, I have a rich heritage. Nonetheless, as a young girl I felt fatigued most of the time, and had many allergies and illnesses. I was confined to bed much of the time and couldn't attend school regularly.

"My father would sit at my bedside and tell me stories. He told me of great women, like Queen Kaahumanu, who helped open Hawaii to Christianity, and Harriet Tubman, once a slave in America, who escaped but returned many times to the South at great risk to bring many of her people to freedom. His stories gave me hope that I, too, might grow into someone more than I was, despite my early infirmities. Years later, author Jack London echoed my father's encouragement when he wrote, 'Life is not always a matter of holding good cards, but sometimes, playing a poor hand well.'

"I suppose I played my hand as well as I could," she continued, taking some macadamia nuts out of her pack and giving me a handful. "When I was seven, my parents heard about a *kahuna kupua* — a shaman — named Papa Kahili. A powerful healer, he was revered by those who knew him, and his reputation grew among those who understood the ancient ways.

"As devout Christians, my parents mistrusted those who spoke of nature spirits. But finally, because I was growing weaker and no one else had been able to help me, their love overcame their fears and they asked Papa Kahili to see me.

"The first time we met, he offered no medicines — nor any of the ceremonial magic that my parents had expected. He just spoke with me quietly. I felt that he really cared about me. That day, though I didn't know it, my healing had begun.

"Later, he brought herbal medicines, and spoke of many things — of the healing power inside me. He told me inspiring stories, painting beautiful pictures in my mind. Papa Kahili took me on many journeys, and each time I returned, I was stronger. But he told my parents, and me as well, that I would never bear children. This dark prediction troubled my parents more than it did me. At that age, bearing children was not foremost on my mind. And besides, we did not believe that any man could know the future."

"Did your parents ever accept him?" I asked.

"Months later, yes. They would call him a 'priest of God,' and they liked how he never took credit for my improvement, but said it was the Holy Spirit that guided and worked through him. He was part of the secret history, like the underground spring that gives life to fields of flowers. The history books would never tell of him; yet, in our smaller world, he was one of the greatest of men.

"At the turn of the century, when I was eighteen, I immersed myself in what I had missed in my early years: I traveled to Oahu and the other islands. I socialized as much as was allowed in those days, and gossiped with the other girls. But eventually, such things lost their meaning to me. I had always felt different from other people, as if I were only a visitor to this world. I had always believed this sense of not belonging was due to my illnesses. But even now I felt like a stranger even among my friends. They enjoyed noisy social gatherings and talking of things that held little meaning for me. I preferred sitting out in the moonlight among the trees and stars," she said, gesturing with her walking stick up toward the towering kukui trees above and around us.

"I thought that maybe all those years confined to bed, in solitude, and all my reading had made me thoughtful about other things, bigger issues. But later it seemed as if I had some kind of foreknowledge, as if I had always known or sensed things others did not see. I began to spend more time alone. When I was nineteen, my father died suddenly. Soon after, my mother's eyesight failed and she suffered a number of ills beyond my powers to alleviate.

"When Papa Kahili returned to Molokai after a decade studying with an African shaman, I asked him to help my mother. By this time he was very old, and his service work in Africa, facing starvation, dysentery, and a host of other afflictions, had taken its toll on him. He told me that Spirit was calling my mother, and that she would soon be free of her painful body — and that he would follow.

"He spoke with my mother and counseled her and, one week after his return, she died quietly in her sleep. After that, I was alone, and I spent every day helping Papa Kahili. Gathering my courage, I asked him if he would teach me the kahuna ways; I told him I felt this was my destiny.

"He was so moved by my announcement that Papa began to cry, because he had seen something within me, but he had to wait for me to ask. So, he adopted me into his family, and into the kahuna tradition.

"Papa Kahili soon departed for the spirit world, but his presence has remained with me always.

"I carried on in his place, helping people he had served; I took special training as a midwife as well. After seeing my parents die, I wanted to welcome more life into the world. In this way, I could participate in the miracle of birth, even if the babies weren't my own.

"Then, in the early 1900s, while in my mid-twenties, I was sent an invitation by an unusual man to meet with a gathering of masters from various spiritual traditions. I felt a deep thrill and inner confirmation. So, despite my fear of leaving my island home, I made the long journey westward across the Pacific by steamship. I was met by a man named Chen at a prearranged site on the coast of China, and I traveled with him to a place called the "roof of the world," where, about a year later, I joined this gathering. It was there I later met a man about ten years my senior — the man you refer to as 'Socrates.' "

"Where did he come from?" I asked. "What was he doing there? And what was his real name?"

"I can tell about my life. Socrates will have to tell you about his own," she said, and would speak no more of it.

Disappointed, I walked in silence, thinking about Mama Chia's past. Until I realized something: "Wait a minute! If you were in your twenties back then...and now it's 1973...then you're...nearly ninety years old! I don't believe it — "

"And I don't keep track of such things," she said. "How old would you be if you didn't know your age? That is all that matters. In any event," she continued, "I later traveled widely on my way back to Hawaii. I'm glad I waited until I could see with the eyes of my heart. Otherwise, I might have passed right by the school."

"What school?" I asked, remembering Socrates' words about a hidden school in Japan or China.

"After Chen arranged for my passage through China," she said, "I visited Siam, now called Thailand, and parts of Indonesia — "

"*What school?*" I repeated.

"A hidden school — "

"How was it hidden?" I asked.

"Not really hidden, but few people could see clearly enough to find it."

"Can you tell me more? I think it's one reason I'm here — to learn its location."

"Now is not the time," she repeated. "You have to learn certain things from your own intuition, your own experience."

We had reached the summit — the highest point for miles around.

"A good place to finish my story," she said, surveying the rain forest far below, "to help establish where we are now, and what we are to do together. As soon as I returned home, to Molokai, in 1910, I was filled with new enthusiasm and energy, ready to call forth miracles, perhaps even heal the lepers.

"What happened next is difficult to explain from my current perspective. But from high hopes and expectations, one risks a fall. And my crises came from a single incident: Soon after beginning my work, I was called upon by a distraught young man whose infant son had suddenly taken ill. He begged me to accompany him to his small cabin. As we hurried to the road, he explained that his child had gone into convulsions, then passed out. The young father was numb with panic, and his wife was beside herself when I arrived.

"They were poor, and isolated, so no other help would be arriving anytime soon. The child was in a bad way — that much was clear." Mama Chia stopped, sat down, and gestured for me to do the same. We sat on an outcropping of rock overlooking the valley below as she related sadly, "I still can't explain what came over me. Despite the *huna* tradition of doing positive work and then stepping back in faith, I felt personally responsible for this child's survival — as if he were the last and only child in the world. I felt I *had* to save him. I did everything within my knowledge and power to help that child; I exerted every last ounce of my will and energy. I prayed, I whispered to him, I called to him. But he died, just the same...."

Even now, many decades later, Mama Chia's eyes misted over. "The child had died in my arms. And something inside me died as well. I believed I could have saved him — *should* have saved him — if only I had studied harder, known more. And perhaps I was secretly grieving for myself, and for the children I would never have, for I remembered Papa Kahili's prediction. I decided that this failure was a sign that I wasn't meant to heal others; that I had chosen the wrong path. This thought consumed me beyond all logic, and — over the protest of those people I had helped, and in spite of the parents' compassionate thanks for my efforts on behalf of their child — I vowed never to practice healing again. I had lost faith in myself and in Spirit.

"I moved to Oahu in 1911, just before the First World War, and started working at the bank. As time passed, I had many dreams of the home and work I had left behind. But I ignored them as mere illusions. It's not without a certain irony, Dan, that I — trained in the *huna* ways — would ignore my own dreams and intuitions. It was not surprising that I developed..." she looked down and gestured toward her body, "this...roundness. I just didn't care enough, or have reason enough, to change. I sank into a secure routine, going through the motions, wearing a smile as I exiled myself from my true life...."

We sat quietly for a little while, until another question popped into my ever-inquiring mind: "Why was your name — when I met you on Oahu — Ruth Johnson?"

"I was getting to that," she said. "The name 'Ruth' I took on as part of my 'other existence.' I no longer felt like the young woman named Chia. As for my last name...it was my married name.

"When least expected, one day in 1918 at the end of the war, I was leaving the Honolulu library when a book slipped from my arms. Before I could even reach down, a handsome soldier appeared from nowhere, scooped up the book, and handed it to me with a smile. He was a tall *haole* stationed there. His name was Bradford Johnson. We began to talk, and never stopped. We were married in 1919. I used to tell him I must have saved his life in a previous incarnation, and that he owed me one.

"After his discharge from the military, he found a teaching post in Honolulu. After that, we lived for some years in a semblance of happiness, or at least a quiet satisfaction. I had a husband and a home. And with both of our jobs, we made do.

"Two years later, I learned I was pregnant. But I lost that baby, and the next. Things changed after that. We just...drifted apart. We separated amicably and Bradford moved east to the American Midwest. He wrote regularly at first, but then his letters stopped.

I stayed on in Honolulu. I missed my home island, but visiting for me was painful — a kind of grieving — so I served people in a safe, conventional way. In one sense, I fit in. But secretly I remained a world apart. Only my dream-life was rich with possibility. In the night I traveled back to the roof of the world, and met with your Socrates. We were quite close those many years ago. But he had traveled, and we had no contact for many years, until one day he found me here — I don't know how. I was working in another bank at the time, and my joy at seeing him was mixed with a terrible shame at what I looked like, and what I had become.

"Yet his eyes showed nothing but affection and gladness to see me, and the effect — I cannot describe its full impact — was a healing as powerful as any I had ever experienced with Papa Kahili. It was the second great healing of my life, seeing myself as he saw me. I felt young again, and beautiful.

"I took a leave from the bank and we journeyed together back to my true home, here on Molokai. I introduced him to those I still knew. We spent some time together before he moved on — he had pressing business elsewhere. So I returned to Oahu, and to the life to which I had grown accustomed. Socrates wrote to me several times over the many years that followed — through the twenties, and the Great Depression, and the Second World War that struck so close to home.

"I lived from one day to the next, until I finally retired when I was seventy-five years old, in 1957. That's when I moved back to my beloved Molokai. Somehow, returning to Molokai with Socrates — and seeing it all freshly, through his eyes — relieved me of a burden I had carried for so many years. Together, he and I began the first in a long line of new and happy memories. That is how it has been with Socrates: although he doesn't take on the mantle of a "healer," his presence and influence have that effect on those around him."

"Yes," I said, remembering...

After a few quiet moments, Mama Chia continued, "I had money saved, and I created a quiet and comfortable home. But few old friends still lived there, and many had passed on. I gardened, and I read, and I volunteered to work with children. And sometimes, when a child was ill, I said or did a few quiet, simple things to help if I could. But it frightened me, somehow, and I held back from anything more.

"Then, six years ago I received a letter from Socrates...."

"That would be 1967," I said.

"Yes. I had no idea how his letter had found me, or why he might be writing after all these years. But his letter, like his visit, changed my life again. I was reminded of things I had forgotten; his words strengthened me, inspired me, and gave me a purpose once again."

I smiled, remembering. "He's good at that. But he can also kick butt when he needs to."

"Yes," she said. "That, too. He's *very* good at 'kicking butt.' And in that letter he told me about you — that you might one day seek me out. Soon after it arrived — and perhaps because of it," she continued, "I returned to the work I was born to do, and have since practiced my work as a midwife and kahuna. I've since welcomed hundreds of infants into the world. And all the while, I've kept my inner eyes peeled for you. So you see, helping you, Dan, is in part a way to show my gratitude for Socrates' love and healing in my own life."

"I love happy endings," I said.

Mama Chia stopped, and turned to me. Her smile faded as she said in a faraway voice, "I hope that when your ending comes, you will be as happy."

I shivered as a cold wind blew in from the west.

CHAPTER 10

The Razor's Edge

Forget about likes and dislikes; they are of no consequence.
Just do what must be done.
This may not be happiness, but it is greatness.

— George Bernard Shaw

BY THE EARLY AFTERNOON, the steep descent gave way to a gentle grade. Following the crest as we were, the rocky trail had shrunk to the width of a balance beam, with a nearly vertical drop of hundreds of feet on either side, and no margin for error. Conversation was out of the question. From the air, I thought, this ridge must look as narrow as the edge of a razor. Fighting vertigo, I forced myself to concentrate on Mama Chia, ten feet in front of me, balancing like a mountain goat as she continued her steady, limping stride. With loose rocks, strewn along the razorback ridge, footing was treacherous, and a misstep would have been disastrous. We continued in this manner, single file, gradually descending to the east, until the path widened, and Mama Chia gestured for us to rest.

With a deep sigh, I removed the knapsack I carried and sat down next to her. Mama Chia reached inside the knapsack and took out two sandwiches. She handed me one. *"Kaukau,"* she said, pointing to the sandwich. "Food."

I bit into the thick slices of bread. "Ummmm, d'licious," I said, my mouth full. And I remarked on the courage she showed, walking along a ridge that gave me, an ex-gymnast, knots in my stomach.

"So you think I'm courageous?" she said.

"Yes, I do."

"Well, maybe so — but that's because I've had some inspiring teachers. I'll tell you about one of them: Many years ago, when I worked as a volunteer at a local hospital, I'd gotten to know a little girl named Liza who was suffering from a rare and serious disease. Her only chance of recovery appeared to be a blood transfusion from her five-year-old brother, who had miraculously survived the same disease and had developed the antibodies needed to combat the illness. The doctor explained the situation to her little brother, and asked the boy if he would be willing to give his blood to his sister. I saw him hesitate for only a moment before taking a deep breath and saying, 'Yes, I'll do it if it will save Liza.'

"As the transfusion progressed, he lay in a bed next to his sister, and smiled, as we all did, seeing the color returning to her cheeks. Then his face grew pale and his smile faded. He looked up at the doctor and asked, with a trembling voice, 'Will I start to die right away?'"

Mama Chia looked over at me. "Being young, the boy had misunderstood the doctor; he thought he was going to have to give her *all* his blood.

"Yes, I've learned something of courage, because I've had inspiring teachers."

After that we ate in silence. Then I lay down for a brief nap. As I drifted off, I thought about that story, and about her story, too. Somehow it gave me perspective about my own life and difficulties, which suddenly seemed small in comparison.

It seemed I had just drifted off when Mama Chia jarred me to wakefulness. "Time to get going; we have to get there before nightfall."

"Are we visiting someone?"

She paused before answering. "In a manner of speaking."

Dark clouds moved overhead, obscuring the sun, now sinking behind the trees, falling toward the horizon. We turned down off the ridge, back into the forest.

"Hurry!" she urged, quickening her pace. "It's getting late." We pushed across the uneven terrain. Another hour passed, and we pushed through tangled branches. The hike had taken the better part of a day, and I was ready to drop. I called ahead to Mama Chia as we descended farther. "We must have walked five or six miles today. Can we take a rest?"

"No rest yet."

A light drizzle started, but the cover of trees over our heads kept us relatively dry.

"I still don't understand how you can move so fast . . . for someone who's so — substantial," I said, nearly running to catch up.

"I can access a lot of energy," she explained.

"How do you do it?"

"A new mother, even though she's very tired, can get up again and again during the night, responding to the calls of a sick child."

"Yes, I guess so."

"That's how I keep going with you," she said.

She continued to set the pace; I followed, slipping occasionally on some moss-covered rocks — up and down ridges, past many small waterfalls fed from the constant runoff on this part of the island, then on through the forest for several more miles.

As we headed up over another rise, and then down, into Halawa Valley, I felt unaccountably refreshed. This feeling of vigor increased as we descended further. Finally, we came to a small clearing, protected on every side by the thick cover of trees.

Rays of sun, low on the horizon, cut through the thick foliage, creating ribbons of light through the greenery. "Make yourself comfortable," she said.

I sat down heavily on a soft bed of leaves, only slightly damp, and dropped her backpack on the forest floor. She remained standing, next to the branch of a kukui tree, staring into space.

I was just lying back looking up through the branches when I heard Mama Chia's voice behind me: "Do you recall what I said before...about shape-shifting?"

"Uh, you didn't really say that much about — " Just then, startled by the loud chirping of a bird, I turned toward her, but she had vanished, and in her place, near where she had been standing, on the low branch of a tree, sat a bird, staring into space, perfectly still, as if waiting for something. "It can't be!" I said aloud. "You're not..."

The bird fixed me with an unblinking gaze; I stared back, waiting for a sign, when Mama Chia's grinning face peeked out from behind the tree trunk. The moment she saw me gaping, her smile turned to laughter. "Dan, I wish I'd had a camera; your expression was priceless."

She stepped forward and winked at the bird; it flew to her shoulder. "So, you thought I'd become a bird."

"I've seen stranger things," I said.

"I expect that you have," she replied. "And many everyday miracles go unnoticed. But people don't physically turn into little birds. Shape-shifting involves the transference of consciousness, a form of deep empathy. Nothing more, nothing less. You feel your way into 'bird awareness.'"

She stroked the little bird, smoothing his bloodred chest and white belly feathers, as he chirped. "This is an *'apapane* bird. He's sort of a pet, and follows me occasionally," she said, touching his curved beak. I call him 'Redbird.'"

"Is he tame?" I asked, recovering from my embarrassment. "Can I hold him?"

"I don't know. You'll have to ask him."

"What am I supposed to do — whistle in bird language?"

She shared a look with the bird, who appeared to roll his eyes in his head as if to say, "Who *is* this guy?"

I reached out slowly, and the semiwild *'apapane* allowed me to stroke his belly.

"I have to admit, that was a nice trick. You had me fooled."

Her expression darkened, like the sky overhead, and she stood. "What we are about to do tonight is not about 'tricks,'" she declared, taking the small bird into her hand. "It's about life and *death.*" Suddenly, she closed her hand tightly on the bird, squeezing him until he lay still and limp in her hand.

In shock, I stammered, unbelieving, "How *could* you?"

It's also about death and *life,*" she interrupted, tossing the little bird up into the air, where he spread his wings, flew up into a tree, and started to sing beautifully, undisturbed by a sudden drizzle, and apparently no worse for wear.

The rain would soon pass, but would this sense of dread?

Mama Chia, unperturbed by my concerns, lay curled up like a mother bear, her eyes closed, her breathing slow and deep.

I rested for about fifteen minutes but couldn't sleep; I was too full of anxiety about whatever waited for me ahead.

When she finally stirred, then stretched, I asked, "Where are we?"

"Inside the boundaries of Kalanikaula, a sacred kukui grove."

"Sacred?" I said, sitting up and looking around.

"Yes. Can you feel it?"

I looked up into the gray bark, light green leaves, and white flowers of the beautiful trees, then closed my eyes and realized that the beauty wasn't so much the look, but the *feel,* of the place. "I feel...a kind of fear — no, not exactly fear, but...awe." Then I added, "Why did we come all this way?"

"You go to a sacred place for a sacred teaching." Abruptly, she stood. "Come. It will soon be dark." Erasing any signs of herself, she turned and walked into the forest. I stood quickly, and followed her example.

"You want to tell me what this is about?" I asked, walking swiftly through the trees, trying to keep her in sight.

"When we get there," she called back.

"Get where?"

Though muffled by the trees, the sound of her voice carried clearly enough. "The burial ground," she said.

"Burial ground? Tonight?" The hairs on the back of my neck stood up — a clear message from my Basic Self that something was coming — and I had no fondness for burial grounds at night.

CHAPTER 11

Tower of Life

Symbolically, then, a tower was originally conceived
as a vehicle for connecting spirit and matter. . . .
The gods must find a way to enter — by force if necessary.

— Sallie Nichols, *Jung and Tarot*

By the time I looked up, Mama Chia was already twenty yards
ahead. I jogged to stay close to her. As we climbed out of the kukui
grove, over the narrow ridge on the way to the burial ground, the
forest changed. As far as the eye could see, in the silver sheen of a
half-moon, lay miles of withered forest — trees that were once
the proud *o'hia* and beautiful *koa,* now gaunt skeletons scarring the
ridges above Wailau Valley. "Deer were introduced here to satisfy
the hunters who kill for sport," Mama Chia explained. "The deer
eat the seedlings, so young trees never grow. Most of the older
trees are dying of dry rot and choked with sticky grass and vines
even the deer won't touch."

We walked upward, over the ridge, and downward, passing
these gnarled patriarchs, the last remains of the dying trees. In the
moonlit forest, Mama Chia began to speak, and her words, like a
powerful magnet, drew me into a new vision of reality. "The

human body is like a tower of seven stories," she said. "This has been known for centuries by inner explorers who have mapped the subtle bodies and energy centers. The Indian mystics called these seven levels *chakras*. Here, let me show you." She stopped, reached behind me into her backpack for a pen and notebook, and, squatting down, she drew a diagram:

THE TOWER OF SEVEN FLOORS

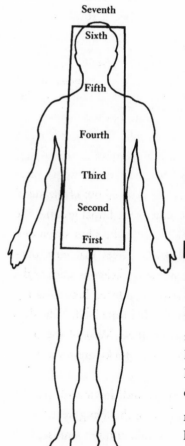

7: TRANSCENDENCE
Pure Spirit; no self remains.

6: UNITY
Pure Light; communion with Spirit.

5: MYSTICAL REVELATION
Pure Inspiration; inner eyes turned toward Spirit.

4: TRANSPERSONAL LOVE
Open heart; ego no longer center. Primary emotion: compassion. Issue: How best to serve.

THE GREAT LEAP

3: PERSONAL POWER
Primary emotions: Anger (tension). Issues: Discipline; commitment; will.

2: SEXUALITY/CREATIVITY
Primary emotion: Sorrow; weakness. Issues: Reaching out; embracing life; energy and relationship.

1: PERSONAL SURVIVAL
Primary emotion: Fear (paralysis). Issue: Looking out for self alone.

As Mama Chia finished, she tapped the diagram with her pen. "This conveys the essence of what you need to know for now," she said. "The tower of life is within you. And each floor has distinct qualities, and each, from the lowest to the highest, represents a more expanded state of awareness.

"The lowest three floors, survival, creativity, and power, are the domain of the Basic Self; it is neither interested in, nor responsible for, the higher floors. Clearing the lowest three floors and dealing with the issues there strengthens the Basic Self.

"On the fourth floor, the realm of the heart, you first make contact with the Higher Self."

"What about the upper three floors?" I asked. "That's where I want to live."

Mama Chia looked up from the diagram, and said only this: "Unless the roots of a tree are deep, it can't blossom; unless the tower has a strong foundation, it will crumble. You've got to clean up the basement before you move into the penthouse. The upper floors are not yet your concern."

I didn't agree, but I let it go for the moment. "What do these words mean, here in the middle?" I asked, pointing to the diagram. "The Great Leap?"

"It refers to the most difficult and wonderful leap any human being can make," she said, "up out of the personal concerns of the lower three floors, into the heart. Once you get to the fourth floor ... the rest is an elevator ride.

"All our external goals and dramas reflect this universal inner quest, and every human being will eventually ascend these seven steps to the soul. The only question is when. For you, I believe it is possible now, in this lifetime."

She started to say something else, but stopped and came around behind me. "Sit down — that's right, get comfortable." She started to rub my shoulders.

"Hey, this is really nice, Mama Chia. If you want, after, I can also give your shoulders a —" Just then my legs began to twitch as she pressed her fingers into a point on my neck. I saw flashes of light.

"Relax as much as you can," she urged, as she pressed her knuckles into my temples — harder, harder. Her voice began to fade as I heard her say, "There are archetypes within the deepest recesses of every human mind...." I felt my eyes closing, then heard the sound of a faraway wind.

I OPENED MY EYES and blinked as clouds of dust blew across a gray plateau, stark as a crater on the moon, stretching for miles in every direction. The wind gusted again, moaning, howling, across the vast expanse. Then my attention focused on a distant object, still too far to distinguish clearly. Was it a tower? Yes, a white tower. And I knew I must go there. By an act of will, and without effort, I felt myself drawing closer. The tower grew larger, until it loomed above me.

Overwhelmed by a wonderful, terrible sense of awe, I found myself outside a window at the base of the tower — the first floor — and I sensed that this floor and those above it were each cluttered with the debris of lifetimes: unexamined issues, symbols, and fears — hidden artifacts in a dusty basement.

As my awareness penetrated the dim light inside, I saw a desolate, empty world, a dust-blown plateau populated only with opponents and enemies.

I soon discovered that each window of each floor offered a different perspective on the world, because inside the second-floor window I viewed a brighter realm of trees and streams and grasses, where couples were engaging in every kind of pleasure, and I was filled with desire.

The third window revealed a world of order, architectural balance, and beauty, where structure rose in a creative crescendo, and people stood straight and tall. On this floor, I spied the gray robot, the Conscious Self, looking out through the window of the senses. And somehow I knew that the Conscious Self had its tiny office here, because this was the highest level it could maintain, in my case.

My awareness then rose to the fourth window, through which I saw all the people of the world, of every color and culture and belief, clasping arms, loving and helping one another and singing in harmony. Feelings of compassion washed over me, and I heard the voices of angels.

My awareness rose swiftly, then, through the upper three floors and, in a wave of rising bliss, I felt, saw, heard, tasted, and smelled far beyond the range of everyday senses, beyond the veils, as I tuned in to subtle energies, to other dimensions and realities, and then — ah, the Light!

In the next jarring instant, like an elevator falling, my awareness dropped down, distracted by alarms from the lower three floors — and I knew that my Conscious Self would be drawn down, again and again, to the issues of fear, sexual energy, and power, until those issues had been cleared.

I remembered, then, with intense longing, that in peaceful, expansive moments of my childhood, I had been invited to the higher floors by angelic energies. I wanted so much to return, because part of me had always known that above the tower, in the place of Light, lay home.

This was my soul's task, my sacred journey: As a Conscious Self, beginning on the ground floor, I needed to find the lights on each rising floor and turn them on, seeing the issues and artifacts there — dealing with them, clearing them. But this would only be possible if I were first willing to see and accept what *is*, rather than clinging to dreamlike illusions.

Returning to a vantage point out on the dusty plain, I once again saw the tower standing before me, stretching up to the heavens, a swirling mist of violet, pink, and gold, and a light shone so brightly above the tower that I couldn't fix my attention there for long.

The next thing I remember, I was sitting, leaning against a tree. My eyes were wide open, but I still saw the tower; then it dissolved as I came back to normal consciousness and saw only the leaves of the kukui tree, blowing in a warm breeze.

I sat, unmoving. Even after all that Socrates had put me through during our time together, I never got used to these revelatory visions. They were not like watching a movie, but rather, like being in the movie, which then became a reality more intense and real than my waking life. Filled with wonder, I took a deep breath and turned slowly to see Mama Chia sitting quietly, not far away. Her eyes were closed.

Finally, I was able to speak. "Whatever you did, I — I understand now, about the tower."

"No, you don't — not yet," she replied, opening her eyes. "But you will." Slapping the notebook shut, she stood, and started down the path. I jumped to my feet, grabbed her backpack, and followed.

"What do you mean, 'not yet'?" I called out.

Her reply was almost lost in the wind. "Before you can see the Light, you have to deal with the darkness."

CHAPTER 12

The Jaws of Fear

Imminent hanging sharpens a man's wits.

— Samuel Johnson

"SLOW DOWN, WILL YOU? What's the hurry?" I called out as I followed on the moonlit trail."

"You'll know when we get there," she said. Her tone was dark, and her answer gave me no comfort. Dodging vines and bushes, I followed as best I could.

Years before, when I practiced gymnastics, fear had been my friendly adversary. Nearly every day, I attempted risky movements — performing twisting somersaults, soaring from the high bar or on the trampoline. I could handle that fear because I knew exactly what I was afraid of, and I was in control. But now, a formless terror spread like a chill inside my chest and belly, and I didn't know how to deal with it. Like my first roller coaster ride as a young boy, I remembered being pulled clickety-clack up the steep ascent, where there could be no turning back, where giggles turned to screams, as we rounded the top. Then the bottom dropped out, and my nerves shredded into terror.

Mama Chia spoke with an urgency I hadn't heard before. "Follow me — this way!" she commanded, turning at a sharp angle. As we headed down, nearer to the burial ground, my mind raced. What could a graveyard have to do with the tower? Filled with foreboding, I fought the urge to run away.

"Walk exactly where I do," she said, her voice muffled by the thick air. "Do not stray from this path; do you understand?"

We broke into a clearing. I saw gravestones ahead, and my solar plexus started cramping as if I'd been punched.

"Why are we doing this?" I managed to say. "I — I thought you were teaching me about the three selves."

Mama Chia took a deep breath, turned to face me, and gestured for me to follow. Her expression was somber, and another wave of fear passed up through my abdomen and chest. This increased my confusion, because I had been in cemeteries before, but I didn't remember when I had ever been this frightened. My Basic Self was petrified, my body numb, as we walked through the ancient burial site. I wanted to tell her, "I don't think I can do this," but I couldn't even speak. I didn't consciously know what was frightening me. But my Basic Self knew; that much was obvious.

The night was warm but my teeth were chattering as I followed Mama Chia on a narrow path through the graveyard. Some of the tombstones stood upright; others were tilted slightly askew. I tiptoed carefully over the graves, until she stopped by a vacant space, and turned to me.

"We are here to confront the darkness of the first floor," she said, "the realm of survival, isolation, and fear. This is a sacred site, protected from the eyes of outsiders. Only kahunas are buried here. Can you feel the power of the place?"

"Y-yes," I stuttered.

"Lanikaula, the guardian, is here, with us now — behind you," she pointed.

I whirled around, but saw nothing, at first. Just an overpowering presence, a force that made me take a step backward. My body turned to ice. It wasn't evil that I felt, but something that could turn me into ashes in a moment without batting an eye — an energy of great compassion, but no mercy.

"He was, and is, a powerful kahuna, and has been here, watching over Molokai, since his death, four centuries ago. We need to ask for permission to be here," she said with great reverence.

"How?"

"Have you ever asked permission to enter someone's home?"

"Yes — "

"Then I advise you to do it, *now,*" she hissed.

She closed her eyes; I did the same. As soon as I closed them, I saw him — right in front of me, in my mind's eye. I snapped my eyes open, and saw only the trees in the distance and the gravestones in this small clearing. I closed them again, and there he was, staring at me with a fierce but somehow loving expression — a large man, wearing some kind of ceremonial Hawaiian headdress. He looked as if he could embrace me or wipe me off the face of the earth. I was reminded of Shiva, the Hindu god — the changer, the transformer, the destroyer.

Silently, respectfully, I asked for his permission to be there, explaining my search. All this happened in a few seconds. He smiled, nodded, and faded out of my vision.

"So be it," I heard Mama Chia say.

Almost immediately, the atmosphere changed. I was bathed in a warm breeze, where before the wind had blown cold on the back of my neck. I opened my eyes.

Mama Chia nodded. "He said you are welcome here," she said.

"I think he actually likes you. That is a very good sign." She reached behind one of the gravestones.

I relaxed. "I'm glad to hear th — " I stopped abruptly as she slapped a shovel into my hand and led me to a bare spot in the earth.

"Time to dig."

"What?" I did a double take.

"Dig here," she said, ignoring my reaction.

"Dig? Here? A hole? Are we looking for something?"

"A grave."

"Look," I said. "I'm a grown man; I make responsible choices. Before I start, I'd really like to know what this is about."

"And I'd really like you to stop talking and start digging," she responded.

"What you are about to do is necessary — based on a Tibetan ritual that involves facing all your fears. If someone who chooses this way is unprepared, it can result in permanent psychosis. I feel you're ready, but there is no way to be certain of it. Are you willing to go ahead?"

There it was: Do or die. Or maybe: Do *and* die. Socrates once told me I could "get off the bus" anytime I wished — if I was willing to let it pull away without me.

"I have to know now, Dan."

I jerked my head toward her as if I'd been slapped. "Oh, uh, well — " I paused to take a breath, and decided to follow the course I'd always set for myself: When a challenge was there, I went for it. "Y-yes," I stammered, "R-ready as I'll ever b-be."

This was about facing fear, so I started to dig. The earth was soft, and the work went faster than I'd expected. As Mama Chia watched, her arms folded, I started with a two-foot-wide channel and lengthened it to about six feet. The hole deepened to three feet, then four. I was sweating profusely now. The deeper I dug, and the more it got to looking like a grave, the less I liked this. And I hadn't been all that enthusiastic to begin with.

My fear expanded, then turned to anger. "No," I said, climbing out of the grave. "I don't have to do this, and I don't want to play mysterious games in graveyards without knowing what it's about. I'm not some puppet! Who is this grave for? Why am I doing this?" I demanded.

Mama Chia stared at me for what seemed like a minute, then said, "Come here." She led me to a nearby gravestone and pointed to the epitaph written there. I peered at it.

The writing was old and faded; I could just make it out:

Remember, friend, as you pass by,
As you are now, so once was I.
As I am now, so you must be.
Prepare yourself to follow me.

I looked over at her face, dead serious. "I think you know who this grave is for," she responded.

I stood and faced her. "I have a choice here," I said.

"You always have a choice," she agreed. "You can start digging, or catch the next surfboard home."

I didn't think she meant it — about the surfboard — but it was clear that if I wanted to continue as her student, I was going to have to see this through. I had come this far. I had to see where it led. Managing a wan smile, I said, "Well, since you put it so nicely." I climbed back down into the grave, and continued digging until she said, "That's deep enough. Hand me the shovel and come on out."

"You mean I'm done?"

"Yes."

"Whoa, I have to admit — that was pretty frightening, all right," I said, climbing up out of the damp grave and laying the shovel nearby. "But all in all, it wasn't too bad." I stretched my weary muscles.

"Lie down here," she said, pointing to a sheet she had placed on the ground next to the open grave.

"Another massage? Doesn't this strike you as a little strange?" I asked.

She wasn't smiling, just pointing. I lay down on my stomach.

"On your back," she said.

I turned over and stared up at her, standing above me. "Now do I play dead, or what?"

She gave me a fierce look. "Sorry," I said. "I guess I'm just a little nervous."

"This is no game; if you offend the spirits here, you'll have a lot more to be nervous about."

Trying to relax, I said, "Well, I could use a rest."

"A long rest," Mama Chia said, picking up the shovel, and bringing its blade down. I threw my arms up protectively, thinking for an instant that she was about to stab me with it, but she planted it firmly into the earth beside the grave. Then she knelt down behind my head, on the edge of the grave, and closed her eyes.

Lying there, I gazed up at her face, upside down in my vision, and pale in the moonlight. For a terrible moment of paranoia, I felt I didn't really know this woman at all. Maybe she wasn't the one Socrates sent me to; maybe she was the Enemy.

She began to speak in a voice that resounded through the burial ground. She spoke an invocation, and I knew this was definitely no game.

"Great Spirit, called by many names," she intoned, "we ask to be placed in the Light. We ask for your protection for this soul. In the name of the One, and with that authority, we ask that any and all evil be cut off and removed from him, sealed in its own light, and returned to its source. We ask that whatever may come be for his highest good. May thy will be done."

The metallic taste of fear rose in my throat. Then Mama Chia slowly began pressing, with her knuckles, along my collarbone, chest, and arms — gently at first, then with increasing pressure. I saw flashes of light again, then heard popping sounds. Then she grabbed my head as Socrates had done, years before. My teeth started to chatter; then the curtain of darkness descended.

I HEARD THE WIND, felt the dust blow in my face, and saw the tower directly in front of me. This didn't feel like a disembodied vision, with my awareness merely an observer. I looked down and saw my body. I was *here*.

Then I was standing in the doorway. The huge door swung open, like a gaping mouth, and I entered, stepping into thin air. I fell, somersaulted, and landed in a heap. I quickly stood and looked around, but barely made out anything in the darkness. "This must be the first floor — the basement," I said. My voice sounded muffled. My clothing clung to my skin, and the dank air and fetid smell of decay was somehow familiar. Find the lights, I said to myself. Be willing to *see*.

Before, I had only looked through the windows of the tower. Did I really want to see what lay inside me, in this, the lowest realm?

"Yes," I answered out loud. "Yes, I want to see." I proceeded forward slowly, reaching out in the darkness. My hand felt something — a large handle, a switch. I pulled it, heard a humming sound that changed to a soft whoosh, and squinted as dim lights slowly began to illuminate the scene in front of me.

Why was it still so dark? As my eyes adapted, the answer came. I had entered the tower and fallen to the first floor, but it somehow contained the night itself and the same burial ground — the graveyard of the kahunas. But this time, I didn't feel welcome at all. And this time, I was alone. I saw the gaping hole of the open grave nearby. My body began to shiver; my mind crossed the border of nervousness, over the raw edge of fear as I was pulled by an unseen force toward the open grave. I turned and twisted, levitating in the air. Then my body became as stiff as a corpse in rigor mortis as I floated down on the sheet next to the grave.

I tried to get up, but I couldn't move. My lungs started pumping, breathing deeper, faster, deeper, faster. Then I heard Mama Chia's voice, from far away: "Your Higher Self is your guardian angel; whatever happens, remember that it will always be with you...."

"Why can't I feel it with me?" I cried out. *"Why do I feel alone?"*

In answer, I heard Mama Chia's recent words echo back to me: "Before you can see the Light, you have to deal with the darkness...."

Then something pushed me. Paralyzed, I had no control; I couldn't resist. I fell, tumbling down in slow motion, landing on my back with a soundless thud in the open grave. A sheet was wrapped around me like a shroud. Then, in a moment of absolute terror, I felt shovelsful of dirt rain down onto me. My heart began to pound wildly in my chest.

I heard the sound of distant thunder. Flashes of lightning exploded in the darkness. Then, as dirt covered me, I heard the voice of Jesus. But he wasn't speaking to me as he cried out from the cross at Golgotha as lightning flashed: *"Why hast thou forsaken me?"*

Then I realized that I was calling out those words. It didn't matter; no one could hear me. The shower of earth had covered my face completely, blotting out any remaining light and muffling the sound of my screams.

Wait! I thought. I'm not ready! I can't! Stop! *I'm not dead!* my mind shrieked.

The earthfall ceased. I felt a stillness and silence more complete than any I've ever known. All I could hear was my labored breathing and pounding heart, like a kettle drum. Alone in the cold earth. Absolute blackness. Isolation. Frozen, gut-ripping fear. I was buried.

An instant of rational reflection: Why did I let this happen? Then that, too, was smothered, and I fell over the edge of madness. My hands, clawlike, desperate, pushed upward against the impossible weight. Soundless screams. Just as the earth began to crush the air out of my lungs, the ground beneath me suddenly caved in, and I fell into an underground tunnel. Clawing wildly, gagging and choking, spitting dirt out of my mouth and nose, I fought my way free of the moist earth.

I began crawling, slithering like a snake, on my belly, up or down — I couldn't tell which — through a long tunnel. I had to get out. Out! Out, out, out, out...repeated itself in a rhythmic babble of dread. I could only squeeze forward; there was no way to turn around. Soon, terrified, I noticed the tunnel was getting narrower, tighter, until I could scarcely move.

Once, as a child, bullies had stuffed me into a burlap sack and threatened to bury me. Instead they stuck me in an old storage trunk. Trapped in the blackness, I went absolutely berserk — drooling, wetting myself, hysterical. My crazy screams must have worried them, so they let me out.

Ever since then, I'd had recurring dreams about being trapped in small dark places. Now my worst nightmares had been realized;

I felt sheer, unendurable terror. I was so afraid, I just wanted to go unconscious, to die.

My eyes stinging with sweat and dirt, I fought on, narrowing my shoulders, but it was no use. I could go no farther. Noises of desperation, fright mixed with cries of anguish, were quickly extinguished. I was stuck, suffocating; I started to scream again, to whimper.

But — was my imagination playing tricks? — I thought I saw a dim light somewhere ahead. I managed to squeeze a few inches more and saw around a slight curve in the tunnel. The tunnel opened slightly, just enough. I inched my way, sweating, with dirt falling in my eyes, toward the light.

Now it was imprinted deep in my body's memory: Whenever I could go no farther, I would remember — just a few more inches, just a few more minutes, just a few more seconds...

I looked up through clouded vision, and thought I saw an opening ahead. Yes, I was sure of it! I reached it and tried to squeeze my head through. I was stuck! Too tight! My head felt crushed by a thousand hands. Desperately, I pushed. The opening started to give, then, suddenly, I burst through. Space! Freedom! Like being born.

Blindly, I pulled the rest of my body out, then fell into an abyss. Below me, impossibly, I saw the gaping mouth and fangs of a gigantic serpent, and I plummeted.

THE NEXT THING I REMEMBER, I was sitting in a room I'd never seen before, huddled in the corner, gripped by paranoia. Outside, the Enemy was waiting for me. All of them. No one understood. I was alone, but I would survive. They wanted what I had — a nearby storage freezer with food. I'd kill the bastards first! On a small table next to me lay cases of ammunition. Surrounded by a variety of carbines and semiautomatics, I wore a shoulder holster with a Glock nine millimeter, its clip holding nineteen rounds, inserted, the safety off. Cradling an AK-47 in my arms, I stared fixedly at the door, waiting for them. They would not take what was mine. I'd kill them first — I'd kill them all.

A canister exploded through the window, and suddenly the room was aflame. In an instant, I was engulfed by searing heat. The air was sucked from my lungs and my skin started to melt. That moment, I remembered a past life as a young girl, hiding in a trunk, hiding from the Huns, burning to death in a room full of flames rather than being raped and enslaved.

The flames shot up and I saw the beginning of the earth: volcanoes exploding everywhere, burning lava searing everything in its path.

And in the heat, the burning heat, I relived every nightmare of my childhood, every fear that had ever visited or forced itself upon me.

I OPENED MY EYES. I was lying on my back at the bottom of my grave, on a sweat-soaked sheet. But I wasn't covered with dirt. Realizing where I was — and that I was holding my breath — I let it out with one huge gasp and began to calm down. Exhausted and disoriented, I was glad to be alive. It was a dream. It was over. I would sit up and climb out. But my legs wouldn't work; neither would my arms.

I heard something above me. "Mama Chia?" I called weakly. "Is that you?" There was no answer — only a soft, padding noise. Someone, or something, was approaching from above.

I heard a soft growl, then the face of a tiger appeared above me. There are no tigers in the rain forests of Hawaii; still, this was a tiger, looking down at me. I stared back; I couldn't take my eyes off it. I'd seen tigers in the zoo — so beautiful, like big pussy cats.

This one was so close I could smell its breath. Oh, please, I said to myself. Let this be a dream.

Completely helpless, I played dead, until it reached down and prodded me, giving me four deep test gashes. I gasped and uttered a brief, stifled cry.

The tiger reached down, clamped its jaws on my arm, and dragged my limp form up out of the grave, then began ripping me apart. I'd felt pain before — searing pain — but now I understood agony.

I tried to go unconscious, to leave my body, to dissociate. But I was attached enough to experience fully the beast tearing open my chest and abdomen, and chewing on my organs.

Shock-borne adrenaline poured through my body. I fell screaming into a cauldron of terror as the huge cat ripped my chest asunder. Then, clamping his jaws around my face and head, the beast tore away part of my face in a seesawing motion, and began to pull my head from my shoulders. Fear is the ultimate pain. It filled my universe, then exploded.

Instantly, the fear, the pain, the tiger, and the universe all vanished. What remained was the deepest peace I had ever known.

CHAPTER 13

Realm of the Senses

God gave us memories
so that we might have roses in December.

— James Barrie

I LAY CURLED ON MY SIDE, next to the grave, my head in Mama Chia's lap. The sheet, soaked with sweat and maybe tears, was twisted beneath me. I sat up, unable to speak, my eyes wide, staring at nothing. I rocked back and forth, hugging myself and shivering. Mama Chia embraced me protectively, stroking my matted hair. "There, there," she said, "It's over now. It's really over."

A few more moments passed. Slowly, I realized I still had eyes, and a face, and a body. I was safe, here in Mama Chia's arms. I relaxed; then my chest heaved, my breathing came out in gasps.

Panting, I gripped her hand and stammered, "It — it f-felt like a tour of hell."

"Only your hell, Dan — we each create our own. You just toured the first floor, the realm of isolation and fear, of mindless instinct to survive at any price.

"Warriors confront their demons head-on; by doing so, you've dissolved them," she said gently.

My breathing finally calmed, and I fell into an exhausted sleep.

WHEN I AWOKE, the sky was light. "Is it dawn?" I asked weakly.

She stood, pointed around us, and said, "What do you notice?"

I stood slowly, drained of all tension, and looked around. A bird landed on a gravestone and began to warble; its song carried up into the blue sky. Lime green lichen and moss decorated the stones; a feeling of peace and reverence pervaded the scene.

"It's different," I said.

"No," she replied. "You are."

"You mean I've cleared fear from my life once and for all?"

"Fear will still arise — but you've changed your relationship to it. You'll know how to deal with it."

"If I weren't afraid of anything, wouldn't that be dangerous?"

"Yes. Fear is a natural response of the body, but you can release the tension; you can breathe through it, and act or remain still — whatever is needed. Fear is no longer your master; now it is your servant. You will see a different world through the windows of the second floor.

"But the first floor isn't only about fear and survival; it's about 'self against the universe,' about the self-protective hoarding of energy for oneself. Now, open and vulnerable, you're ready to bring that energy fully into life, to share it in relationship."

"You mean I'm ready to find door number two?"

"You already found it. Here, in my arms, when you cried." As she said this, Mama Chia began to shimmer, and she dissolved into the air, right in front of my startled eyes. Then, everything around me vanished. I saw a fleeting image of the tower, and found myself standing in a sylvan glade, on the second floor. I was certain of it.

BUT WHAT DOES IT MEAN? I asked myself as I surveyed the rich meadow, bathed in soft sunlight and cool breezes. This could have been an idyllic forest in lusty old England. "Strange," I caught myself saying out loud. "Why did I think of the word 'lusty'?"

Then, gradually, I became increasingly aware of energy, building up in my whole body — more energy than I had felt in years. I felt so awake and alive! I had to move, to let the energy fly. Sprinting through the forest, I felt as if I could run miles and miles. I leaped, I turned handsprings, and then I ran some more.

Finally, I rested in the warm sunshine. Somehow, the seasons had changed. Spring was, as they say, in the air, when a young man's fancy turns to....

The energy started building up again as a familiar, uncomfortable pressure in my loins. Mama Chia had said the second floor dealt with "energy in relationship." That meant creative energy, sexual energy. But what was I going to do with it?

Out of nowhere, I could hear the words of Socrates, from years before. "Every human capacity," he said, "is amplified by energy. The mind becomes brighter, healing accelerates, strength increases, imagination intensifies, emotional power and charisma expand. So energy can be a blessing..."

Yes, I said to myself. I felt all those things.

"But energy must flow somewhere," his voice continued. "Where energy meets obstructions, it burns — and if energy builds up beyond what a given individual can tolerate, it demands release. Anger grows into rage, sorrow turns to despair, concern becomes obsession, and physical aches become agony. So energy can also be a curse. Like a river, it can bring life, but untamed it can unleash a raging flood of destruction."

"What can I do now?" I asked, talking to the air.

Memories of Socrates' voice echoed from the past: "The body will do whatever it has to in order to bleed off excess energy. If it isn't spent consciously, in creative endeavors and physical activity, the urge for release will take the form of angry outbursts, or cruelty, or nightmares, or crime, or illness, or abuse of alcohol, tobacco, other drugs, food, or sex. Blocked energy — and the desire to feel release — is the source of all addictions. Don't try to manage the addictions; instead, clear the obstructions."

I was so distracted by the building pressure that I could barely concentrate. The energy continued to grow, demanding release. I could run some more, or I could make something — yes, something creative. That's it, I decided. I'll make up a song. But all I could come up with was "There once was a beaut from Killervy, whose body was nubile and curvy; a man found her there, in her lace underwear, and..."

I couldn't think of a damn ending; I couldn't think at all. I just wanted a woman. Any woman.

I was about to take care of this surging desire myself when I remembered that this level of the tower was about bringing energy into *relationship*. Damn! How was I going to manage that?

The next instant, I found myself in a cave — not a gloomy, foreboding cave, but what appeared to be a luxurious bedroom. Thick rugs overlapped on the floor; rays of sunlight bathed the room through a natural skylight. The entrance, concealed by a thick growth of small trees and bushes, rendered the place completely invisible to outsiders.

In the center of the cave stood a sleeping platform, covered by a thick bed of soft leaves, a few feet off the cave floor. I heard the comforting trickle of a lovely waterfall pouring into a miniature pond and smelled the sweet fragrance of wildflowers.

Then I gasped with surprise and excitement as a soft breeze blew over my entire body; a sensual wind, a beautiful ghost, caressed me with invisible hands. I felt a oneness with the earth and with all my physical senses, now amplified. I was so happy to have this body, to feel the body, to be the body completely.

All I needed was a loaf of bread, a jug of wine, and — I could forgo the bread and wine, but...

What was that? Was that voices I heard? Female voices?

I peered out through the leafy door and saw a picture of an artist's dream. The picture would be titled *Maidens of Spring.* Three young women, all voluptuous, were laughing, running under some apple trees, their rosy cheeks reflecting the reddish glow of the fruit above. They wore dark, flowing skirts and low-cut, frilly blouses that highlighted their feminine charms. I felt like a hormone-crazed teenage voyeur as I spied on these women.

Two of them waved good-bye, and the third, a flaxen-haired angel whose green eyes flashed in the sunlight, stopped, looked left and right, then, smiling, ran straight for my hiding place. "Oh, damn!" I said to myself, half afraid she was going to find me here, half afraid she wasn't.

She slipped into the cave and saw me standing there like a love-starved lunatic. Her eyes met mine, and grew larger.

I started to speak but my voice was stilled as she fell into my arms.

My mind was empty, except for three words: *Thank you, God.*

Then passion overtook me completely. We laughed, we cried, we were lost in each other. I don't know what happened to our clothing; whatever got in the way of our union was cast aside. Time passed; I don't know how long. We lay there, cradling each other, completely spent, asleep in each other's arms. But not for long.

When I awoke, she stood over me, draped in a robe made of flowers. Her angelic face, surrounded by silken hair, shone in the soft light. She let the robe slip off her shoulders; her luminous skin shone like a baby's.

For a moment, questions arose — Who was she? Should I be doing this? — but only for a moment.

She knelt down and kissed me on the forehead, then on my cheeks, then lips and chest and worked her way down from there. Sexual energy coursed through me as Bacchanalian images appeared in my mind — rites of fertility, earthy, sensual — and deep within me I heard and felt the pulsating beat of drums. She kissed my body until it hummed and throbbed to the beat of the drums, and my questions fell away like leaves on a windy day.

I drew her to me, we cradled each other, and I returned, in kind, what she had given until there was no her, and no me. Only us, then one, and wild, mindless sexual play I had experienced in rare moments when my mind was free and my heart open. But now it intensified manyfold — not just because she was a desirable woman, but because I was so... open. Having just faced the blackest death, I was now fully capable of celebrating life and all that it entailed. The monk inside had succumbed to Zorba the Greek. Nothing stood between me and life.

The feeling intensified many times over, as waves of pleasure pulsated, not just in my loins, but in every cell in my body. But I was taken slightly aback, just for a moment, when I noticed that I was making love with a man. And the man was me — Dan Millman!

I sat up with a shock. I looked down at my hands, my legs, my breasts: I was a woman! I was her! I felt her insides, her emotions, her energy — soft, but strong. The energy flow was different than I was accustomed to, and in my state I could sense a larger, more sensitive emotional aura. It felt so good — like a completion.

Then we embraced again, and I lost all sense of separation. I was her, I was him, I was her and him.

I stayed with the body. I trusted it. Undulating in ecstasy — naked, free of any assumed limits, I was skin; I was nerves and muscle and blood — tingling, pulsing, delighting in the realm of the senses. Shapes, touching, moistness, sucking, stroking, feeling, throbbing, smooth, warm — I entered the moment completely.

We were locked in a passionate embrace building like a wave, racing toward the shore, when she vanished. No! my body cried out, frantic with wanting. Overcome by both desire and sorrow, I felt the snares of the second floor.

I sat up, panting, ready to explode, the energy churned inside me like a caged panther, pacing madly, seeking escape. I reached out to pleasure myself when again something stopped me — an understanding that I had to *use* the energy, circulate it. I didn't fight my body; I didn't deny it — instead, I breathed, deeply and slowly, until the force of desire spread from my genitals upward, up my spine, up my torso, to the tips of my fingers and toes and the center of my brain.

My mind became light. A gateway had opened; energy rose up from the earth itself, through my spine. Energy that had been trapped below now flowed upward. I tasted the purity of being, the body electric, singing.

But I wasn't fully prepared for this, or practiced, and despite the good intentions of my Conscious Self, my Basic Self apparently had other ideas. The waves continued, growing stronger, until I could stop it no longer. Images passed through my mind like nocturnal fantasies, body parts, moaning sweetness, and suddenly, inevitably, though not of my own accord, the tidal wave, the pulsing wave, crashed into the shore, and subsided.

After a time, I stood up. I felt a gentle, unaccountable sorrow, a sense of loss — not in my mind, but in my body. Perhaps it mourned the loss of that brightness, that energy. She was gone; the object of my desire had vanished, as all objects do. Now, there was only the wind blowing through the trees. Until Mama Chia appeared, snapping me back to whatever reality I could hold on to in my present state.

I stood naked before her; she could see my body and my mind. She knew everything about me, and all that I had just experienced. And she accepted me completely, as I was. Any traces of embarrassment dissolved. I stood before her, naked and unconcerned, like an infant. There was no shame in being seen, no disgrace in being human.

On the first floor, I had broken the thread of fear; now, I broke the thread of shame. For the remainder of my days, however long that might be, I would allow life energy to flow freely through me. I would learn how to use it wisely, choosing where to channel it, celebrating life, but not exploiting it. I was not a master of energy, by any means, but I was a willing apprentice.

Two things happened in quick succession: I saw that I was now fully clothed, and then my surroundings, the cave and glade beyond, flickered and vanished. Neither of these things surprised me.

MY NEXT MOMENT OF AWARENESS found me standing somewhere high in the mountains. The wind whistled loudly past rocky crags and granite crevices, almost drowning out Mama Chia's voice behind me.

"Come," she said. "Time to move on."

"I was alone before; why are you with me now?" I asked, my voice echoing strangely from the cliffs facing over a deep gorge.

"You had to be alone before; now you're in relationship with the world. Besides, we're in dream time, and I wasn't doing anything. Welcome to the third floor."

As we hiked upward, I gathered strength from the ground beneath me, from the stones, the trees, the wind — flesh of my flesh. No longer at war with my body, accepting my physical imperfections, trusting my own human nature, I felt a closer connection to the earth.

We found a small lake, and swam through the cool waters, then lay on warm rocks to dry. My body opened to the natural world; I felt the lake's serenity, the river's power, the stability of the mountain and the lightness of the breeze.

Mama Chia looked over at me. "In this place, I feel what you feel, I am what you are," she said. "You just shape-shifted — at least the beginning stages."

"I did?"

"You did. Shape-shifting begins with a gesture of imagination — a sense of curiosity and wonder: What would it feel like to be a mountain, a lake, a bird, a stone? Later, you learn to resonate with the different frequencies of these elements or beings. We humans have the power to do this because, after all, we're made of the same spirit.

"And speaking of shape-shifting, I think you know I was attuned to you in that cave on the second floor. Quite an adventure!" she said. "Made me feel young again."

"You'll always be young," I said.

"You're right about that," she said with a smile. "Until the day I die..."

"You'll probably outlive me at this rate."

She looked deep into my eyes. Her gaze made me sad, though

I didn't know why. I saw the love in her eyes, but also something else — a concern, an intuition — but I couldn't fathom what it meant.

Mama Chia quelled my preoccupations as she led me forward, reminding me of the lessons of the second floor: "You created your own experience, Dan, just as you did on the first floor; you experienced exactly what you needed. The energies are the same for everyone; the experience is different. Each of us chooses how to respond to and channel our energy. Some hoard it; others squander it. The warrior channels the flow of life energy like a farmer irrigating his crops.

"On the first floor, alone and fighting for survival, you fearfully hoard the energies of life like a lonely miser with his money; because the energies are blocked, they cause pain.

"On the second floor, you are in a relationship with life, with other people; both the male and female principles are active and in balance.

"The second floor is not just about sex; it's about celebrating the energy of life. Energy is Spirit; energy is sacred. You have a choice before you each day, whether you will master the energy of your life, or squander it. The myth of Pandora's box is not about letting mischievous imps or demons out of a container; it is about ways of dealing with life energy. When energy is thrown away without purpose or wisdom, you feel an instinctive loss of life, a sense of sorrow."

"Why sorrow?" I asked.

"Fear is the shadow side of the first level," she answered. "Sorrow is the shadow side of the second."

"And the third?" I said. "What do you have planned for me now?" Mama Chia only smiled.

— CHAPTER 14 —

Flying on Wings of Stone

Nothing real can be threatened. Nothing unreal exists.
Therein lies the peace of God.

— A Course in Miracles

MAMA CHIA LED ME through a rocky canyon, through a short tunnel of stone, then up onto a narrow trail along the spine of a razorback ridge. "First, let's sit here a while."

She closed her eyes. Not wanting to disturb her with questions, I did likewise. There wasn't much else to do up here, or so I thought.

When I opened my eyes again, I could see the sun setting over the far western edge of wherever-we-were. Then Mama Chia opened her eyes and handed me some corn and nuts from her never-empty backpack. "Eat this; you'll need it."

"Why do I have to eat? This is a dream, isn't it? Come to think of it," I noticed, "this floor feels more real than the others. This *is* some kind of vision, isn't it?"

Ignoring me, she said, "The third level is about power, not power over others — that is the negative side — but personal power over the impulses of the Basic Self and the desires of the ego. Here you find the challenges of self-discipline, clear intention, duty, responsibility, focus, commitment, will — those things that most apprentice humans find so difficult.

"Now that you've cleared the second level and have a sense of connection to others, your attention is freed for higher impulses. It will be easier for you to take others' needs into account as well, though true altruism doesn't exist on the third floor. Your Basic Self is still in control, but better disciplined. What you do for others, you do out of duty and responsibility. Love still eludes you."

"Are you saying I can't really love?" I asked, disturbed by her statement.

"There are many kinds of love," she said. "Just as there are many kinds of music or films or food or drink. There is first-floor love, limited to the most primitive, even abusive, sexual encounters. Second-floor love is vital and pleasure-oriented, and the partner is also taken into account. Third-floor love is an artful, conscientious practice."

"I asked you about love, and you keep talking about sex."

"Until you are settled on the fourth floor, that's about it."

"Go on."

"No need to; you get the idea."

"What about the love on the higher floors?"

"Let's deal with that when you're ready," she said. "Just understand that the world mirrors your level of awareness. Like attracts like — and people whose home base is the first floor are attracted to first-floor kinds of music, books, films, drink, food, sports, and so forth. The same is true of the second and third floors. Until your awareness rests stably on the fourth floor, in the heart, your motives are ultimately self-serving."

"You're saying that when my awareness resides more on the fourth level, I won't be so self-centered?"

"We're *all* self-centered, Dan — the question is, which 'self' are you centered on — the Basic Self, Conscious Self, or Higher Self? And as your awareness rises from the third to the fourth level, you perceive and experience a different kind of life — you begin to live as a Higher Self in the world."

"What does all that have to do with where we are now?" I asked, gesturing toward the mountain peak on which we stood.

"I'm glad you asked me that," she said. "Because I have a small task for you that may help you rise beyond the third floor," she said, as we stepped around an outcropping of rock, and she pointed to a narrow, level but rocky path about fifty yards long.

"What am I supposed to do?" I asked.

"For starters, walk along this path as far as you can; see what there is to see."

"Door number four?"

She shrugged and, with a graceful gesture, pointed the way.

I walked carefully down the narrow ridge but stopped short as I came to the edge of a precipice — a chasm that dropped to nothingness as far as I could see — maybe two thousand feet — straight down. I took a step back from the dizzying height and looked across the gaping abyss at the opposite cliff wall about thirty feet away. It looked as if the mountain peak had been sliced in half by a gigantic knife.

Suddenly behind me, Mama Chia said, "The door is there." She pointed across the abyss to a small ledge, little more than an indentation on the opposite cliff wall. But, sure enough, there did appear to be a doorway there. "All you have to do is leap across."

I gauged the distance again — obviously too far to jump. I looked to Mama Chia to see if she was joking. Her face showed no sign that she was.

"That's not possible," I argued. "First of all, it's twenty-five or thirty feet away, and I'm no long jumper. And even if I made the jump, if I miss that narrow ledge I'll slam into the cliff face and slide down to oblivion."

"You're not afraid, are you?" she asked.

"No, not really — but I'm not stupid, either. It's suicidal."

She looked at me with an irritating, know-it-all smile.

"I said no. Not a chance."

She waited.

"This isn't a dream now," I bellowed. "And I'm not a bird."

"It can be done," she said, pointing across the chasm.

I started to walk with her back up the trail, shaking my head. "This isn't about fear, Mama Chia — you know that. It would just be foolish. I don't mind testing my limits, but if I overreach myself here, I'm dead."

I felt her hand even before it touched me. The hairs shot up on my neck and goose bumps raised; then I saw a flash of light. Something changed. Or had it? Everything looked the same, but felt different. I was still standing there, talking to her. "Is this a dream?"

"Everything is a dream," she replied.

"Yes, but I mean right now — "

"There is always the chance," she added, "that you may fail."

"If I fail, will I really die?"

"Your physical body will be undamaged, but the pain will feel very real, and, yes, a part of you will most certainly die."

"But if this is some kind of vision, I can do anything I want."

"It's not that simple," she replied. "You'll only be able to accomplish what you believe you can; it will still take a leap of faith to make it across. This isn't really a test of your body, but of your mind — your focus, discipline, intention, and, in a way, your integrity, or integration.

"You've already accomplished much — a lifetime's worth for many. Only accept this challenge if you truly wish to go on. Ask yourself: Can you *will* yourself across? This is your test of personal power. And there," she pointed again across the chasm, "lies the path to the fourth door."

I stared once more out over the chasm. I tested my abilities in this realm by jumping up off the ground, expecting that I might float upward like a man on the moon — but I came down with a physical sensation of landing, and rose no higher than I normally would in my physical body. I tried once again with the same result. This is crazy, I thought. Maybe it was a trick, a test of my judgment. She had said that if I jumped and failed to make it across, "a part of me would die." Maybe I wasn't supposed to accept a foolish challenge. What if I declined to jump at all? Yes, that must be it, I thought. It was a test not of my will, but my judgment. I turned to Mama Chia, but she was gone.

Then I heard someone calling for me. "Dan! Help me, please! Help!" I looked across the chasm, to where the voice echoed from, and saw Sachi, clinging to the ledge near where I was to land. It was impossible. Surely a trick of the mind. Then she cried out again. I could see her slipping, struggling to climb back to the ledge.

"This isn't fair!" I said. "It's not real!"

"Daaaaannnn!" Sachi yelled desperately. She got a foothold, then lost it.

Then I saw the tiger. It padded along a narrow ledge on the cliff face, moving toward Sachi. She didn't see it.

"Please!" she called again. I had no choice; I had to try. I ran quickly back along the narrow path for about thirty yards, turned, and took off.

As I picked up speed, doubts assailed me: What am I doing? I don't think I can make this. Then a kind of cold anger over-whelmed me. Not anger *at* anything or anyone — just a forceful energy, like a giant wave that washed away everything in its path. Nothing was going to stop me.

Accelerating, focused completely on my goal, I raced toward the precipice. With a surge of power, my mind forgot past and future, tigers and chasms, as I locked on to one thing: the landing spot. I leaped.

For a moment, floating through space, I felt that I might not make it. Still aloft, I soared through space and time, as if in slow motion. I felt the heavy pull of gravity taking control. I felt myself dropping. Then, something happened. Maybe it was my imagination, but drawing on everything within me, I *willed* myself across. I felt like I was flying.

An instant later, I landed with a very real thud, and, rolling into the shallow cave, I hit the wall. The tiger was running toward us. Dazed, I stumbled to the edge, reached down, and pulled Sachi up. Then, just as the tiger leaped, I pulled her through the doorway.

I must have hit the wall pretty hard. As soon as I was through the door, I passed out.

I AWOKE, MOMENTS LATER, in the dim light. My arms were bruised, and my head hurt. I hurt all over. I looked at my wrist; it was crooked — broken. Then, as I watched it, the wrist straightened itself out, the bruises disappeared, and the pain subsided. I closed my eyes for a few moments.

WHEN I OPENED THEM, I was sitting up, on an old sheet, beside an open grave at the sacred burial site of the kahunas.

The morning sun struck Mama Chia's face, bathing it in a rosy glow. But she looked pale and drawn, in spite of it. Noticing me staring, she smiled wanly, and said, "The last few days have been challenging for both of us. If you think *I* look bad, you should see yourself."

She handed me a plastic bottle with water. "Drink this."

"Thanks." I was parched, and gratefully I took the water. Since my episode out at sea, I had little tolerance for going thirsty. That fear, at least, seemed to remain in the depths of my Basic Self.

When I finished drinking, Mama Chia stood. "Come on. We have a long walk back." We said a respectful good-bye to Lanikaula, and though he didn't appear to us in the daylight, I could feel his presence and blessing.

On the way back, it struck me: Although I'd cleared the third floor and shown sufficient discipline, focus, and self-mastery to find and pass through the door to the fourth floor, my vision had ended then; I had not made it to the fourth floor. I had some sense of what had happened, but I asked Mama Chia for her view.

She gave a simple, straightforward response: "You aren't ready yet. Your psyche rejected it. You came back."

"So I blew it," I said.

"That's oversimplifying, but it comes out to about the same thing."

"So what do I do now?"

"Well...your training with Socrates helped you with the first three floors, as I've said. You are prepared to enter the fourth level. It may happen at any time. But, you see, the Great Leap requires that the Conscious Self, the ego, loosen its grip. That may be what's holding you back."

IT SOON TURNED DARK. We camped in the rain forest. Tomorrow, I thought, we would have an easy walk — a couple of hours, then home.

Soon after starting out in the morning, however, we came to the foot of a dramatic waterfall, thundering down from a shelf forty feet above.

"You know," I said, gazing at the pounding falls, "Socrates once cautioned me about getting too fascinated with inner stuff, with visions and such. He said it can lead some people, who aren't too grounded to start with, into all kinds of illusions. He used to tell me, even after sending me on an inner journey, to keep the lesson and throw away the experience.

"So, I've been thinking — maybe all these visions don't prove anything conclusive. It's a lot easier to be courageous or uninhibited or disciplined in a dream than in real life. I don't really feel that different. How do I know anything's really changed?"

"What you've gone through was much more than a dream, Dan. And keep an open mind about what you call 'real life.'"

"But I still want to prove something to myself."

Mama Chia smiled and shook her head, amused. She gazed intently at me for a few moments, then looked at the falls, then back at me. "Okay," she said. "You need to prove something? Go meditate under that waterfall for a while."

I took a fresh look at the falls, and considered it. That was a lot of water crashing down; it wouldn't be like taking a shower. "Yeah, I can do that," I answered casually. I had once seen something like this in a martial arts movie. "Okay. I accept. I'll do it for twenty minutes."

"Five hours would prove a lot more," she said quickly.

"Five hours?" I'd drown in five hours! Or suffer brain damage!"

"I'd say the damage has already been done."

"Very funny. Okay then, maybe I'll try it for one hour, but that's tops. I don't even know if *that long* is possible." I removed my shirt and started to take off my sneakers, then decided against that and left them on. I stepped carefully on the slippery, moss-covered rocks, and climbed out under the falls.

I was almost knocked flat by the force of the water. Fighting my way in, almost slipping twice, I found a place to perch on a flat rock and sat, pushing my spine straight up under the force of the deluge. The water was cold, but in this climate bearable. I'm glad the weather's warm, I thought, before the liquid avalanche drowned out all thoughts.

Through sheer determination and a growing tension headache before everything got numb, I stuck it out for what felt like an hour, so I figured that at least twenty minutes had passed. I was preparing to call the game on account of rain, when something stopped me. Maybe it was courage, or determination, or discipline. Or just pigheaded stubbornness.

Years before, when the coach would ask for fifteen handstand push-ups, I would always do twenty. I'd always been like that, as long as I could remember. So, while I kept wanting to get up, get out, quit — something kept stopping me. Somewhere in the back of my mind (the front of my mind had already drowned) was Mama Chia's challenge, playing again and again like a mantra: five hours, five hours, five hours...

In my years of gymnastics, my Basic Self had been trained to respond to the word "challenge" by pulling out all the stops. I felt a surge of energy rising up through my abdomen and chest as I realized that I was actually going for the full five hours — and that I might just make it. No, I *would* make it, do or die.

Then the world disappeared in the deluge, and my mind was no more.

SOMEWHERE IN THE POUNDING, in the noise that grew fainter and farther away, I heard the wind, and I saw a white tower flying toward me in my mind's eye.

I found myself in a tiny room. Acrid smells filled the air, odors of sewage and decay, partly masked by strong incense. I recognized the dress — colorful saris even in this terrible poverty. There was no mistaking this place. I was somewhere in India.

Across the room, a woman, wearing the garb of a nun, was

caring for a bedridden leper, his face a mass of sores. He had a deep, oozing fissure in his cheek, I noted with disgust, and he was missing an ear. He was dying. Recoiling from the sight, revolted by the smells, and the sickness, I stepped back, in shock, and withdrew.

The wind gusted; I leaned against a worn brick wall in an alleyway in France, just off the narrow rue de Pigalle. A gendarme was picking up a drunk, covered with vomit, smelling of the gutter, to help him into the police van. Disgusted, I stepped back, and this scene, too, receded in the distance.

The wind blew again; I sat like a ghost, unseen, on the bed of a teenage boy, in an upper-class suburban house in Los Angeles. He was sniffing powder up his nose. Stupid kid, I thought. Get me out of here.

The next instant, I stood outside a hut in Africa, gazing through the doorway at a very old man, moving painfully, trying to get some water into the cracked mouth of a young baby, its belly swollen, its ribs almost breaking through the skin.

"What is this?" I cried out loud, feeling like I was back in hell. "What do these people have to do with me? Take me away from here! I can't take this; I don't want any more."

My eyes closed, I shook my head back and forth to shut out these people and their suffering. I heard a voice calling me, growing louder. "Dan . . . *Dan.*"

I BECAME VAGUELY AWARE of Mama Chia, under the waterfall with me, pulling my arm, yelling, "Dan . . . come out! You're finished."

"Y-y-you c-c-an say th-that again," I managed to mutter. Shivering like a waterlogged cat, I staggered out from under the falls, shaking my head, trying to clear it. I stumbled and fell upon some soft grasses and lay in the sun, letting the rays slowly seep into my chilled body. When I finally opened my eyes, Mama Chia was sitting quietly nearby, gazing up at the falls.

"I'm not taking a shower for a year."

Mama Chia opened a mango and handed me a piece.

"I think I grew gills," I said. "Anyway, that proved something, didn't it?"

"Yes it did: While you were slowly drowning, I hiked to my house, took a nap, visited with a friend, walked back, and enjoyed this mango." She tossed the large pit into the bushes. "It proves something all right — that one of us is a fool."

Mama Chia laughed so sweetly that I had to chuckle, too.

"You have a good spirit, Dan. I knew that from the start. Socrates helped you to turn on the lights of the third floor. So now, when your Conscious Self resolves to do something, your Basic Self knows your level of commitment and gives you the energy to accomplish it. I'll grant you that much," she said with solemnity. "You have become a human being."

"That's all?"

"Quite an accomplishment — it means you've done some housecleaning on the first three floors. You've gotten in touch with your body, with the world, and with your humanity."

"But, something happened under the waterfall," I told her. "I saw all these poor people — the sick, the dying. Somehow, I think I visited the — "

"Fourth floor," she finished for me. "Yes, I sensed that — down at the cabin, in my sleep." She nodded, but her eyes looked a little sad.

"Well, what did it mean? Did I pass?"

"The waterfall, yes. The fourth floor, no."

CHAPTER 15

In the Service of Spirit

I slept, and I dreamt that life was all joy.
I woke, and saw that life was but service.
I served, and discovered that service was joy.

— Rabindranath Tagore

AS WE WOUND OUR WAY DOWN into the forest, I asked, "What exactly happened to me back there...leaping that chasm...and then under the falls?"

Limping upward, Mama Chia responded, "For you, as well as for many others, the third floor remains an arena of battle. Cluttered with issues of discipline, commitment, will, and self-restraint, that level of awareness represents a 'finishing school' for the Basic Self.

"Until you clear the issues at this level and attain a secure foundation of self-mastery, your life will reflect a constant struggle to bridge the chasm between knowing what to do and actually doing it. The warrior has mastered the Basic Self — trained it — so that wants and needs are the same, no longer in opposition.

"In leaping the chasm, you showed a strong will; otherwise, you would have fallen into the abyss."

"What would have happened then?"

"A long climb back," she said, smiling.

"Was Sachi really there?"

"In your mind, yes — I believe she represents the daughter you left waiting for you back in Ohio."

Pangs of regret, responsibility, and love washed over me as Holly's little face appeared in my mind. "I should be getting home to see her."

"Of course," she agreed. "But will you bring her a whole father, or a man with unfinished business?"

Again Soc's words resounded inside me: "Once begun... better finish."

"Have you finished here yet?" Mama Chia asked, reading my thoughts.

"I still don't understand what happened to me under that waterfall — "

She cut me off. "You made a tremendous jump across that chasm. But an even greater leap awaits you."

"To the fourth floor?"

"Yes — into the heart."

"Into the heart," I repeated. "Sounds kind of sentimental."

"Sentiment has nothing to do with it," she said. "It's a matter of physics — *meta*physics. And you *can* make this leap, Dan. But it will take great courage, and great love. These qualities are coming alive in you. It all begins with a longing, as you've described." She paused, then added, "I know you better than you know yourself, Dan. All your adventures are nothing more, and nothing less, than Spirit searching for Itself. Your Higher Self, filled with love, waits for you with infinite patience. That meeting is so close. I only hope I live to see — " she caught herself and stopped in mid-sentence.

"What was that? What did you say?"

Mama Chia looked as if she were about to speak, but only resumed her limping gait, and continued talking where she left off. "You'll meet your Higher Self the moment your awareness rises out of the sea of personal concerns, into the heart. You don't have to climb the mountains of Tibet, you see, for the kingdom of heaven is *within,*" she reminded me. "In and up — the heart and above — it's all there."

"What about the floors above?"

"I've told you — one step at a time. Find the heart, first; then the higher floors will take care of themselves, but you'll be too busy loving and serving to care."

"I don't know if I'm cut out to play 'Saint Dan.'" I grinned at her. "For one thing, I like cookies too much."

"Well," Mama Chia replied, smiling. "When you leap into the heart, you'll truly *love* cookies. I know *I* do!" She laughed, but said nothing more for a while, as if to let all she had said sink in, the way a gardener lets water seep down deep, toward the roots.

I looked up and around; clouds passed over the midday sun. Mama Chia's words had reached in and touched someplace deep inside me. We continued walking, in silence, until more questions arose in my mind.

"Mama Chia, I've seen people who have unusual powers or abilities. Does that mean they are on the higher floors?"

"People sometimes have gifts due to the work they have done in past embodiments. But most often — unless they've cleared all the debris below — they only have a 'temporary pass' to the upper floors to contact those points of energy and see through those windows."

"How about spiritual masters?"

"The awareness of a genuine master is present at birth, but

may remain latent — even through periods of inner turmoil and confusion — until it blossoms rapidly, catalyzed by an event or teacher. Great masters can access the higher floors — indeed, they manifest great love, energy, clarity, wisdom, charisma, compassion, sensitivity, and power — but if they haven't also mastered the lower floors, they end up absconding with the money or sleeping with their students."

"I'd sure like to experience those upper floors."

"Certain mystical techniques and substances have been known for centuries to provide glimpses of the upper floors. These are best treated as sacred, rather than recreational, activities; they can be useful as 'previews of coming attractions.'

"Many well-intentioned, lonely, bored, or desperate people generate spiritual experiences through a variety of techniques," she continued. "But then what? What have they got? They return to their normal states more depressed than ever.

"Spirit is always here, always with us, around us, inside us. But there are no shortcuts to this realization. Mystical practices generate heightened awareness, but if experiences aren't grounded in a responsible life in *this* dimension, they lead nowhere." She said, following a turn in the path.

"Those who seek to escape the world through spiritual experiences are barking up the wrong tree, because their search only intensifies the sense of dilemma that motivated the search in the first place.

"The desire to rise above the boredom, fleshiness, and morality of this world is natural and understandable. But those who practice self-involved techniques to distract themselves from the dilemmas of daily life are going to ascend the ladder only to find out it's leaning against the wrong wall.

"You meet the Higher Self not by imagining colored lights or doing lovely visualizations, but by accepting its will — by *becoming* the Higher Self. This process cannot be forced; it happens of its own accord.

"Daily life is your training ground," she continued. "Spirit gives you everything you need, here and now. You evolve not by seeking to go elsewhere, but by paying attention to, and embracing, what's right in front of you. Only then can you take the next step on whatever floor you are working.

"And then," she said, stopping and facing me, "when the lower floors are clear, something very subtle and exciting occurs: Your motives make a rare and dramatic shift from *seeking* happiness to *creating* it.

"Ultimately, it comes down to service. Jesus said, 'Whoever would be the greatest among you is the servant of all.' This, Dan, is the way to the heart, the path up the inner mountain. And mark my words: One day you will serve others not out of self-interest or guilt or social conscience, but *because there's nothing else you'd rather do.* It will feel as simple and pleasurable as seeing a wonderful film that makes you feel happy and wanting to share it with others."

"I don't know if I'm capable of making service the center of my life. It still sounds like a burden."

"Of *course* it does," she replied, "because you are still seeing it from the third floor. But from the fourth-floor window, from the eyes of the heart, convenience, personal comfort, and satisfaction are no longer the center of your existence. You will look forward to getting up each day just to help another soul, another part of your Self."

Mama Chia stopped talking as a rainsquall made our footing treacherous. Stepping over twisted roots, it was hard to walk and talk at the same time. I concentrated on my mud-caked sneakers beating a squishing cadence on the wet earth and thought about what she had told me. We sloshed down through the rain that saturated the forest, passing several small but scenic waterfalls along this narrow, slippery path.

Later, when the path widened, Mama Chia glanced back at my concerned expression and said, "Don't be too hard on yourself, Dan. Accept where you are. Trust your Higher Self. It has been calling to you since you were a child. It brought you to Socrates, and to me. Accept yourself and just serve. Serve out of duty until you can serve out of love — without attachment to the results.

"And when you'd be content to spend a hundred lifetimes — or an eternity — serving others, you no longer need to practice a way, because you've *become* the Way. Through service, 'you,' the Conscious Self, evolve into a Higher Self, even while in human form."

"How will I know when this happens?" I asked her.

"You won't. You'll be too ecstatic to notice. As the ego dissolves into the arms of God, the mind dissolves into the will of God. No longer trying to control your life or make it work out in a particular way, you stop living and start *being lived*. You merge with a larger purpose — you become the Way by getting out of the way."

"I don't know," I sighed. "It sounds impossible."

"When has that stopped you before?" she asked.

"You've got a point," I said, smiling.

"When Joseph de Veuster was a boy," she added, "if someone had told him he would spend his adult life ministering to lepers on the island of Molokai, he might have thought that impossible, too. But Joseph became Father Damien, and when the lepers were abandoned here to languish and die, he found his calling, and served them for the rest of his life. And look at Mother Teresa, and Mahatma Gandhi, and — "

"And look at you," I interjected.

We passed down into the rain forest, down toward my cabin,

and a needed rest. The tree roots and rocks gave way to grass, leaves, and damp red earth. We were both weary, and we traveled in silence. I concentrated on breathing slowly and deeply, keeping my tongue on the roof of my mouth, allowing my Basic Self to circulate and balance the energies that flowed through me. I inhaled not only air, but light and energy and spirit.

I became aware of birdsong, and the ever-present trickle and rushing of streams and waterfalls — runoff from the rain showers — drew me once again into the beauty and mystery of Molokai. But the nagging issue of service, certainly a weak link in the chain of my life, kept rising to the surface of my mind, pressing me.

"Mama Chia," I said, breaking our silence, "when you mentioned Father Damien or Mother Teresa, I realize how far I am from anything like that. The idea of working with lepers and serving the poor just doesn't appeal to me at this point in my life, though I know it would be a good thing to do."

Without turning around, she answered. "Most of humanity joins in your sentiments. Good deeds are done for many motives: On the first floor, you only find self-service; on the second floor, service always has strings attached; on the third floor, it is motivated by duty and responsibility. I say again: True service begins at the fourth level, when awareness resides in the heart."

We walked on into the afternoon, stopping once to pick some mangoes. My hunger only slightly appeased, I felt glad for the remaining nuts from Mama Chia's pack. She just nibbled, content with her meager fare.

"Keep eating like this," I said, "and you'll soon be slim as a model."

"A model what?"

"A model saint," I said.

Mama Chia shook her head but said nothing.

As we resumed the final leg of our downward hike, I asked

Mama Chia, "How am I ever going to make that leap you talk about? After all, I have a job, a family to support, and other commitments. I can't just go around giving things away, spending all my time volunteering."

"Whoever suggested you should? And where have you gotten all these ideas?" she asked. "Maybe from the same place I did." Slowing her pace, she added, "When I was young, ideals didn't come any higher. I was going for the Holy Grail, and that was that. Not a day passed that I didn't feel guilty reading books and studying and attending films — while other children were starving in other parts of the world. I vowed that I would help those less fortunate than I.

"During my travels, my ideals suffered a rude jolt. I had saved some money to give to the poor and, as soon as I got off the train, a child approached me. She was beautiful — neat and clean, with shining teeth in spite of her poverty. She begged politely, and I was happy to give her a coin. Her eyes lit up.

"Then three more children ran up and, smiling graciously, I gave each of them a coin as well. Then I was surrounded by fifteen children, and that was just the start. Everywhere, there were more children begging. I soon ran out of coins. I gave away my carrying bag and an umbrella; I gave away nearly everything but the clothes I was wearing and my air tickets. Soon, if this kept up, *I* would be begging, too. It had to stop somewhere; I had to learn how to say no without hardening my heart. It was painful for me, but necessary. I had not taken vows of poverty — and neither have you.

"Yes, this world needs more compassion. But we all have different callings. Some people work in the stock market, others in the prisons. Some live in luxury, while others are homeless. Some people deliberate on what type of imported marble to place in their indoor pools, while others starve on the streets as Christmas shoppers pass by. Does this make villains of the rich or saints of the poor? I think not. Complex karmas are at work. Each of us plays our role. Each of us is born into life circumstances to challenge us and allow us to evolve. A beggar in this life may have been wealthy in another life. Inequity has always existed, and until the awareness of humanity rises *at least* to the third floor, it will continue.

"Over time, I have come to accept my guilt about being comfortable and having enough to eat," she explained. "Otherwise, how can we take a bite of food while others starve?"

"How do you deal with these feelings?" I asked.

"The question itself reveals your awakening heart," she said. "The way I deal with such feelings is I act with kindness to the people in my immediate surroundings. I accept the role I have been given, and I suggest you do the same. It is all right for a peaceful warrior to make good money, doing what he or she loves, serving other people. All three elements are important. It is all right to hurt, to love, to be happy, in spite of the difficulties of this world.

"Find your own balance. Do what you can, but take time to laugh and enjoy life. Yet, at the same time, know that as your consciousness rises up into the tower of life, your lifestyle naturally changes. Your needs simplify; your priorities — how you spend your time and money and energy — all change."

"I have high ideals, too — I want to get closer to them. I want to change."

"The first step to change, as I expect Socrates showed you, is accepting your reality right now. Honoring your process. Compassionate self-awareness leads to change; harsh self-criticism only holds the patterns in place, creating a stubborn and defensive Basic Self. Be gentle with yourself as you would with a child. Be gentle but firm. Give yourself the space to grow. But remember that the timing is in God's hands, not yours."

CHAPTER 16

Dark Clouds on a Sunny Day

Here are the tears of things; mortality touches the heart.

— Virgil, *The Aeneid*

I HAD ABSORBED ALL I COULD. My mind and heart felt rested, but not my feet — I was running on empty, carried downhill more by momentum than by any reserves of energy. Again it struck me as incredible that this elderly woman could have traveled all these miles, limping every step of the way.

When we were nearing home, Mama Chia led me onto another trail than the one I'd remembered. A few minutes later, we came to a small cabin next to a cascading stream. As we approached from above, I could see a Japanese rock garden with one large rock — an island in a sea of raked gravel — with a bonsai tree arching up in perfect balance with the whole. Above it lay another terraced garden with vegetables and flowers.

The cabin itself stood up off the ground on stilts. "We sometimes get a lot of water," she explained without my asking, as we went up three log steps and inside. The decor was perfect Mama Chia: a long, low futon couch, green carpeting like the forest leaves, a few paintings on the walls, and some *zafus* — meditation cushions — and assorted pillows.

"Can I make you some iced tea?" she asked.

"Sure," I said. "Need any help?"

She smiled. "While this is tea for two, it doesn't take two to make tea. The bathroom's over there." She pointed to my left as she headed into the kitchen area. "Make yourself at home. Spin a record on the turntable if you want."

Coming out of the bathroom, I looked for the record player and found an old windup model, an antique.

When she brought out the tea, and some fresh papaya slices, Mama Chia seemed so peaceful — at home in her environment — as if she'd been here all the time instead of taking me on a grueling cross-country hike.

When we finished our tea, I cleared our plates and washed them. She said, "We're only about a mile from your cabin. You could use a rest, I imagine."

"Yes," I said. "You, too."

Mama Chia knelt, Japanese style, on a cushion in front of me, and gazed directly into my eyes. "I feel I've come to know you well these past few days."

"The feeling's mutual," I replied. "You amaze me! Socrates sure knows how to pick friends." I smiled.

"Yes, he does," she added. I guessed she was referring to me.

"You know, it's strange — we've only known each other for a few weeks, but it feels like so much longer."

"Like a time warp," she said.

"Yes, exactly — and it's going to take some time for me to take in all that I've learned," I told her.

She paused for a moment, then said, "Perhaps that's what life is for — giving us time to take in what we learn."

We sat quietly for a while, enjoying the serenity of her house and the pleasure of each other's company. I was suddenly moved to tell her, "I feel so grateful to you, Mama Chia."

"Grateful to *me?*" She laughed, apparently thinking this humorous, or even absurd. "I'm happy for you; gratitude is a good, wholesome feeling. But when you're thirsty and someone gives you water, are you grateful to the glass, or to the person who gave you the water?"

"To the person," I answered.

"I am only the glass," she said. "Send your gratitude to the Source."

"I will, Mama Chia, but I also appreciate the glass."

We shared a laugh, and then her smile faded slightly.

"There's something I feel I should tell you, Dan, just in case...." She hesitated for a moment. "I have trouble with blood clots — a high risk of strokes. The last one gave me this limp, this shaky hand, and some sight loss in one eye. The next one, if it happens, will be fatal."

She said all this matter-of-factly. I felt a shock pass through my whole body. "The doctor who originally diagnosed it," she continued, "and the specialist who offered the same diagnosis, said I could function normally — except for the usual cautions — but that my life expectancy at this point is very tenuous. There's not much they can do — they give me some medicine, but..."

She sat still, as I absorbed this. I stared into her eyes, to the floor, and into her eyes again. "Did those 'usual cautions' the doctors told you include not pushing yourself to your limits on endurance hikes?"

Mama Chia smiled at me with compassion. "You understand why I didn't tell you before."

"Yes — because I would never have gone." Feelings of anger, concern, sorrow, fear, tenderness, betrayal, and guilt washed over me.

A heavy silence settled on the room. "You said the next stroke would be fatal. Don't you mean *might* be fatal?"

She hesitated, then said, "I sense I'll be dying soon. I can feel it. I just don't know exactly when."

"Is there anything I can do?" I finally asked.

"I'll let you know," she said with a comforting smile.

"With everything you know — all your rapport with your Basic Self — can't you heal yourself?"

"I've asked myself that question many times. I do what I can; the rest is up to God. There are some things one must accept. All the positive thinking in the world will not grow back a missing leg; my problem is like that."

"That friend I told you about — the one who died," I reminded her. "When he first found out he was ill, he felt all those things people feel in his situation — the shock, the denial, the anger, and, finally, the acceptance. Well, it seemed to me that he had an opportunity either to conquer the illness — to commit all his time, energy, and will to healing — or, to accept on the deepest level that he was going to die, surrender, make peace with the world, take care of business, and somehow use it for his evolution. But he never did...." I thought about him and a sadness settled over me before I continued, "He did what I imagine most people do. He wobbled with halfhearted efforts, never really fighting death *or* accepting it, until the end. I was...disappointed in him." It was the first time I had ever shared that feeling with anyone.

Mama Chia nodded slowly. "I've seen people completely surrender to death, and in that surrender, they were healed. In my own case, I will fight for my life even as I accept my death. In the meantime, I'm going to live — really live — until I die. Whether it's today, tomorrow, next month, or next year. That's all anyone can do."

She looked at me, and I think she could sense how much I wanted to help her. "There are no guarantees in this life, Dan. We live the best way we know how. I listen to and trust the messages from my Basic Self. But sometimes, in spite of everything — " She finished her sentence with a shrug.

"How do you deal with that — with knowing that at any time..."

"I don't fear death; I understand it far too well. But I do love life. And the more I laugh, and the more I play like a child, the more energy my Basic Self gives me to keep right on dancing." She squeezed both my hands. "You've given me some fun *and* some laughs these last few days."

My eyes started to sting. I embraced her and she welcomed it.

"Come on," she offered, "I'll walk you home."

"No," I said quickly. "I mean — I can find my way. You get some rest."

"That sounds appealing," she said, stretching and yawning.

As I turned to go, she called to me and said, "Now that you mention it, there is something you can do for me."

"Name it."

"I have some errands to run, people to see. You can assist me, if you like — carry my extra pack, that sort of thing. You doing anything tomorrow?"

"I'll check my appointment book," I said, happy for the invitation.

"Okay," she responded. "See you then. And, Dan, please, don't be troubled by this." Then, with a little wave, she turned away. I walked slowly down her front steps to find the path back to my cabin. As I headed down through the trees, I wondered if I would ever feel the way she did — helping others just for the love of it, with no thought of myself. Then something else occurred to me. Was it possible that Socrates sent me here not only to receive her help but to somehow help her as well? It struck me once again: He worked at a service station — a *service* station.

By the time I got back to the cabin, I realized two things: first, that Socrates had sent me here to learn how to serve; second, that I had great debts to repay.

THE NEXT MORNING, bright and early, I heard the loud chirp of a bird right in my ear and felt a tiny weight on my chest. I opened my eyes cautiously and saw Redbird, Mama Chia's friend, the *'apapane* bird. "Hello, Redbird," I said quietly, not moving. He just tilted his head, gave another chirp, and flew out the window.

"I see the early bird got here before me," said Mama Chia as she entered, gesturing toward a tree just outside, where he was singing.

"I'm ready to go," I said, tying my shoes, remembering that I'd promised myself not to act gloomy and maudlin around her. "What's first?"

"Breakfast." She handed me some fresh bread, still warm.

"Thanks!" I said, sitting on the bed and munching. "By the way, I've been meaning to ask you, does this cabin belong to you?"

"It was a gift; Sachi's father built it a few years ago."

"Pretty nice gift," I said with my mouth full.

"He's a pretty nice guy."

"So when do I meet him?"

"He's away, working on a building job. There's not much construction on Molokai these days, so when an opportunity comes up..." She shrugged.

"Where's Sachi been?"

"She ought to arrive any minute now. I said she could come along."

"Good; I've developed a real fondness for that little lady."

Sachi walked in, blushing as she heard this.

Mama Chia picked up one backpack and pointed to the one I was to carry. I reached down. "Whoa, this is heavy," I said. "Is it full of rocks, or what?"

"As a matter of fact, it is," she said. "I wanted to bring Fuji and Mitsu some choice stones — for their rock garden. And the exercise will do you good."

"If it gets too heavy for you, I can carry it," Sachi volunteered with a dimpled smile.

"If it gets too heavy, you can carry *me.*" I grinned back, and turned to Mama Chia. "Isn't Fuji the photographer you told me about? Didn't he and his wife just have a baby?"

"Yes. Now he does landscape gardening — works at Molokai Ranch. Very handy with tools."

FUJI AND MITSU greeted us with warmth and courtesy and introduced us to their infant son, Toby, who was unimpressed, and sound asleep. "He arrived only a few weeks ago, with Mama Chia's help," Fuji announced.

"The same is true of me. I hope his trip here was easier than mine," I said, grinning at Mama Chia and slipping the rock-filled pack off my back. I placed it on the porch with a thud.

"Rocks for your garden," Mama Chia explained to Fuji while I stretched my arms and shoulders. Then she offered, mostly for my benefit, "If they aren't exactly what you want, we'll be glad to take them back."

One look at my expression and they all laughed.

Their cabin was filled with bric-a-brac and memorabilia, neatly arranged on many shelves. I also noticed beautiful photos of the surf and trees and sky — probably taken by Fuji.

Surrounded by trees on every side, with hanging plants decorating the walls, it was a beautiful house, a happy house. We heard the squalls of the baby, waking up hungry.

While Mama Chia attended to Mitsu and her newborn son, Fuji offered to give us a tour of the garden. "Mitsu and Fuji have a beautiful garden," Sachi said enthusiastically.

And so they did: cabbages, cornstalks, rows of beans, and squash. I saw taro root greens sticking up through the soil. Bordering the garden on one side was an avocado tree, and, standing sentry on the other, a fig tree. "We have good potatoes, too," Fuji said proudly.

I could feel nature spirits all over the place; my Basic Self, I noted, was speaking to me more clearly lately — or maybe I was just listening better.

After our tour, we sat on the porch and talked about landscaping, photography, and other things, until Mama Chia emerged.

When we said good-bye, Fuji made a point of shaking my hand. "If there's ever anything I can do for you, Dan, please ask."

"Thank you," I said, genuinely liking this man, but not expecting to see him again. "My best to your family."

Mitsu waved from the house, her baby at her breast, and we turned down toward the road.

"We're going to town," Mama Chia told me. "I borrow Fuji's pickup when he doesn't need it."

She squeezed herself behind the wheel of his little truck and moved the seat back so she could breathe. I slid into the passenger side; Sachi hippity-hopped onto the back of the truck. "Hold on for dear life!" Mama Chia yelled out to Sachi, who squealed with delight as we bumped down the dirt and gravel road, to the two-lane main highway.

"Going to town," I thought. "What a phrase." I hadn't seen

much of civilization since I walked down that beach toward Makapuu Point, weeks ago.

THE TOWN OF KAUNAKAKAI, on the southern side of the island, reminded me of a false-front Hollywood set — a three-block-long commercial section, with buildings of wood, brick, and faded paint. A sign at the outskirts read "POP. 2,200." A wharf extended far out into the harbor of this seaside town.

Mama Chia went into a store to shop. I waited outside with Sachi, now entranced by a gift shop window display next door. As we stood there, I glanced over at four Hawaiian boys in their late teens as they approached and stopped next to us. Ignoring my Basic Self's "something is wrong here" feeling, I didn't pay much attention to the youths, until one of them suddenly turned and snatched the flower out of Sachi's hair.

She turned to them and said indignantly, "Give me that!"

Ignoring her, he started to pull off the petals, one by one. "She do love me, she don't love me, she do, she don't . . ."

Another boy said, "Who cares — she ain' big enough to do nothin' but — "

"Come one, give me the flower," I said, in a show of bravado. Or stupidity. They turned and glared at me; now I'd done it.

"You want dis flowa?" said the biggest of the boys, six inches taller and about a hundred pounds heavier than I, with a beer belly and, I suspected, some muscle under his flabby bulk. "Why don' you take it?" he challenged, grinning at his friends.

As the other young toughs surrounded me, Beer Belly suggested, "Maybe you wanna wear it?"

"Nah," said another punk. "He ain' no queer; I think she his girlfren'," he said, jerking his head toward Sachi, now embarrassed, and a little afraid.

"Just give me the flower," I commanded — a big mistake.

Beer Belly stepped up and shoved me backward. "Why don' you take it from me, *haole,*" he spit.

I grabbed his wrist with one hand, and tried to get the flower. He threw it away and took a swing at me.

The blow glanced off my scalp as I hurried to avoid it. I didn't want to hit this guy; I just wanted to get Sachi out of there. But it had gone too far. I shoved him with all my might. He stepped backward, tripped on a beer can, and fell awkwardly. One of his friends laughed. He came up furious, mad enough to kill, and fully capable of it. But just then, the storekeeper ran out in time to save my skin.

"Hey! You boys!" he yelled as if he knew them. "No fighting around here if you want to come back, you hear?"

Beer Belly stopped, looked at the storekeeper, then glared and pointed at me. With his finger jabbing the air like a knife, he said, "Next time, bro', you dead meat."

They sauntered off. "You just made a bad enemy," the storekeeper said to me. "What were you fighting over?"

"This," I answered, picking up the flower and blowing it off. "Thanks for chasing them off."

Shaking his head, the storekeeper went back inside, muttering, "Crazy tourists."

As Sachi came over and touched my arm, I realized I was shaking.

"Are you all right?" she said.

"I'm fine," I answered, but I knew that was only partly true. My Conscious Self had stayed cool, but my Basic Self was shaken up. Ever since I was a little boy, I'd been told, "Never fight! Never fight!" by an idealistic mother in a not-so-idealistic world. I had no brothers, and I just didn't know how to cope with physical confrontations. I wished Socrates had taught me some of his martial arts.

"I'll be okay," I repeated. "How are you doing?"

"Okay, I guess," she said.

I handed her the flower. "Here — nearly as good as new."

"Thanks." She smiled, then her smile faded as she watched the rowdy gang walking away. "I've seen them before, they're just bullies. Let's go inside. I think Mama Chia's done."

As I carried the groceries to the truck, I looked around for those boys and resolved that I would learn how to defend myself, and protect others, if necessary. The world could be a dangerous place, and people weren't always peaceful. If it wasn't a street punk, it might be someone else; I couldn't ignore this area of my life. If that storekeeper hadn't come out...I vowed never to let something like this happen again.

"You two have a good time?" Mama Chia asked as we got into the truck.

"Sure," I said, giving Sachi a look. "I even got to make some new friends."

"That's good," she said, smiling. "After we put away these groceries, I'm going to introduce you to some special people."

"That's nice," I said automatically, not having the faintest notion about who they might be.

By late afternoon, our errands complete, we returned Fuji's truck. Sachi hopped out of the back and, with a "See you later," took off with a running start, up the dirt road.

"The keys are in the truck," Mama Chia called to Fuji with a wave of her hand, and we started up the path to her cabin. I insisted on carrying most of the groceries — three large bags —

but left Mama Chia with one small bag. "I don't see why I have to carry this bag," she whined loudly. "After all, I am an important kahuna shaman and your elder — and you could easily have carried this in your teeth, or between your legs."

"You're right," I said, shifting the middle bag so I could see over it. "I am truly a lazy person, but I know you'll free me from my slothful ways."

"The slothful warrior," she said. "Definitely has a ring to it."

I helped her put the groceries away, then headed out the door. I heard Mama Chia call after me, "I'll meet you at your cabin in about an hour."

CHAPTER 17

Courage of the Outcast

If I am not for myself,
Who will be for me?
And if I am only for myself,
What am I?
And if not now, when?

— Hillel, *Sayings of the Fathers*

As it turned out, this hike was nearly as far as the previous one, but in the opposite direction. But this time we hitched a ride part way with a Molokai rancher up a long dirt road, nearly to the ridge, and from there stayed on the trail until it dropped steeply, then climbed again.

Every time Mama Chia started breathing hard, I asked her how she was doing. When I did this the fourth or fifth time, she turned to me and, as close to angry as I'd seen her, said in pidgin English, "You ask how I do one mo' time and I sen' you back home wida swift kick! You understan'?"

In the late afternoon, as we cleared a final rise, Mama Chia stopped quickly and put her arm out to halt me. If she hadn't, the next moment I might have had a short-lived career as a bird. We stood at the edge of a cliff, dropping a thousand feet down to a

dramatic view: clouds floated past a blue-green sea, and an albatross glided across the surf far below. My eyes followed the soaring
bird until I noticed some kind of settlement, surrounded by tall
palms. "Kalaupapa," she pointed.

"What's down there?" I asked.

"A key to the elevator."

I only had a moment to consider this before Mama Chia
turned and stepped down into a hole in the earth. As I caught up
with her, I found my footing on some kind of hidden stairwell in
the cliff face. It was steep and dark. We didn't talk at all; it was all
I could do to stay on my feet.

As she led me down the stairwell, we were treated to a dancing play of light and shadow as beams of sunlight penetrated the
holes in this winding staircase. Finally, we emerged from the cliff
wall into the sunlight and descended farther, relying on handholds
to avert a fatal plunge to the rocks below.

"Only a few people use this trail," she said.

"I can understand why; are you sure you're okay — "

Shooting me a fierce glance, she interrupted. "There's a mule
trail, but it has twenty-six switchbacks. This is quicker."

We said nothing more until we rounded a steep bend and
walked down into a broad valley between the higher ridges, cliffs,
and the sea. Lush foliage and rows of trees bordered a small settlement ahead, and, beyond that, sand and water. Orderly rows of
barracklike apartments, simple and sparse, and some small cottages stood by the sea amidst the palm trees. Even in this sheltered
cove, the settlement was more spartan than luxurious — more like
an army outpost than a vacation getaway.

As we drew closer, I saw a few people outside. Some older
women were working in what looked like a garden area; a lone

man, also older, was working with some kind of grinding machine — I couldn't quite make it out from this distance.

As we drew near and walked through the settlement, people looked up at us, with friendly, but often scarred, faces. Most turned toward us and nodded, smiling at Mama Chia — apparently a familiar face here — while others remained intent on their work. "These are the lepers of Molokai," Mama Chia whispered softly as a warm drizzle passed over us. "First abandoned here, out of fear and ignorance — quarantined and left to die — in 1866. In 1873, Father Damien came here and served this community until he contracted the disease and died sixteen years later," she said, "when I was seven years old."

"He died of the disease? It's catching?"

"Yes, but it's not easy to catch; I wouldn't worry about it."

Despite her assurance, I *was* worried about it. Lepers! I had only seen them portrayed in biblical movies, when Jesus performed healing miracles. *He* wasn't concerned about catching anything — after all, he was *Jesus*. But I was ... worried.

"There are conventional doctors who serve these people," she said quietly as we walked into the village. "Though the lepers are, for the most part, full-blooded Hawaiians, many are Christian and don't believe in *huna* medicine. But there are a few I counsel. These are the people who have had unusual dreams or experiences — things their doctors don't understand."

Trying not to stare, I saw a few people with obvious disfigurements. One woman sat in a chair, reading; she had only a tiny stump for a leg. A man was missing both hands, but that didn't stop him from grinding something with an electric tool. "He makes fine jewelry — silver dolphins," Mama Chia said.

More people emerged from their bungalows as word of our

arrival spread. The youngest person I saw was in his forties. His head was bandaged. An older woman with scraggly hair came up to us and smiled; there were sores on her face, and she was missing a few teeth.

"Aloha," she said to Mama Chia, then to me. Her smile was bright, friendly, and curious. To Mama Chia, she gestured with her head toward me. "Who dis *kane* [man]?"

"He's come make *kokua* [help]," Mama Chia replied in her best pidgin English. "My packhorse," she added proudly, pointing to me and generating a beaming, if fragmented, smile from the crone. "Maybe he stay a few days, help out — only way I get these good looking boys out of my hair," she added for good measure. The old woman laughed and said something in Hawaiian. Mama Chia raised her eyebrows and laughed heartily at this.

Puzzled, I turned to Mama Chia. "Did you say we're staying a few days?" That was the first I'd heard of it.

"*We're* not staying; *you* are."

"You want me to stay here a few days? Is this really necessary?"

Mama Chia looked at me a little sadly, but said nothing. I felt ashamed, but I had absolutely no desire to stay here.

"Look, I know you mean well, and it might be good for me and all that, and there are people who like to do this kind of thing — like that Father Damien — but the truth is, I've never been the type to hang around hospitals or soup kitchens. I respect people who do those things, but it's just not my calling, you know?"

She gave me that look again, and the silent treatment.

"Mama Chia," I tried to explain, "I jump backward if someone *sneezes* in my direction. I don't like to hang around illnesses. And you're suggesting I stay here and mingle with lepers?"

"Absolutely," she said, and turned toward a cottage down on the beach. I followed her to some kind of central building, a dining hall.

Just before we stepped inside, she said to me, "Except for the doctors and priests, visitors here are not common. Your eyes will be a mirror for these people; they are sensitive to you. If you look at them with fear and revulsion, that is how they will see themselves. Do you understand?"

Before I could answer, we were surrounded by several men and women who rose from their food, obviously glad to see Mama Chia, who took her backpack from me and brought out a package of nuts and what looked like some kind of fruitcake she had baked. "This is for Tia," she said. "Where's Tia?"

People were coming up to me, too. "Aloha," said one woman, touching me lightly on the shoulder. I tried not to shrink back, and I noticed both her hands looked normal. "Aloha," I answered, smiling on the outside.

Just then, I noticed people making way for a woman, the youngest I had seen here — in her late thirties, I guessed. She looked about six months pregnant. It was a sight to watch her and Mama Chia attempt to hug. Smiling, they approached each other warily, leaning sideways, like two blimps trying to dock.

Tia actually looked very pretty, even with a crippled hand and a bandaged arm. Mama Chia then gave her the cake. "This is for you — and the baby," she said.

"Mahalo!" Tia said, laughing, then turned to me. "This is your new boyfriend?" she asked Mama Chia.

"No," she declared. "You know my boyfriends are better looking — and younger." They laughed again.

"He insisted on coming here to help out in the garden for a few days; he's a strong boy and was glad to hear the rule that volunteers work until dark." Mama Chia turned toward me, and with a flourish said, "Tia, this fella named Dan."

Tia hugged me warmly. Then she turned back to Mama Chia:

"I'm so glad to see you!" With another hug — they had it down now — she walked off to show Mama Chia's cake to the others.

We sat down to eat. A woman offered me a tray of fresh fruit; she was very gracious, but I couldn't help noticing that she had only one eye on a scarred face. I wasn't very hungry, and I was about to tell her so, when I looked up into her one eye. And we made some kind of contact; her eye was so clear, and bright — for a moment, I think I saw her soul in there, and it looked just like mine. I accepted what she offered. "Mahalo," I said.

LATER, WHILE MAMA CHIA and I sat alone on two old wooden chairs, I asked her, "Why was that woman Tia so grateful for a cake?"

She laughed, "That wasn't about the cake — though I do make wonderful cakes. She was grateful because I've found a home for her baby."

"You what?"

She looked at me as if I were very dense, and she was going to have to move her lips very slowly. "Did you notice that there are no children here? None are allowed, because of the disease. Children born of lepers do not usually have the disease, but they are more susceptible, so they cannot live here. That's perhaps the saddest thing of all, because these people have a special affection for children. Two months before the birth of a child, the woman must leave, have it elsewhere, and say good-bye."

"You mean Tia won't see her child — she has to give it up?"

"Yes, but I found a family not too far away. She'll be able to visit her child; that's what she's so happy about." Mama Chia stood abruptly. "I have people to see, and things to do, so I'll see you around."

"Wait a minute! I didn't say I was staying."

"Well, are you?"

I didn't answer right away. We walked in silence, down toward some bungalows, and the beach area a few hundred yards further. Then I asked, "Do you come here to teach them?"

"No, to learn from them." She paused, searching for words. "These are ordinary people, Dan. Were it not for their disease, they would have been working in the cane fields, selling insurance, practicing medicine, working in banks — whatever other people do. I don't want to idealize them; they have the typical problems and same fears as anyone else.

"But courage is like a muscle; it gets stronger with practice. People don't test their spirit until they're faced with adversity. These people have faced some of the hardest emotional as well as physical battles: Ostracized by fearful people, they live in a village without the laughter of children. The word 'leper' has become synonymous for 'one who is turned away from,' — a pariah — abandoned by the world. Few have faced as much, and few have shown such spirit.

"I'm attracted anywhere there's a lot of spirit. That's why I've taken special interest in these people — not as a healer — as a friend."

"Aren't they the same thing?"

"Yes," she smiled. "I suppose they are."

"Well, I guess I can be a friend, too. I'll stay — but just for a few days."

"If you grit your teeth and just put in your time, you'll have wasted it. This week is about opening your heart — as much as you can."

"A week? I thought you said a few days!"

"Aloha," she said, tossing me a bottle of sunscreen and heading off to visit a nearby settlement. Shaking my head, I turned and walked back down toward the row of cottages, thinking about adversity, and about spirit.

I found my way to the main hall, and entered. It turned out to be the infirmary, full of strange smells and people in beds, behind curtains. A very lean, emaciated man about Mama Chia's age took me by the arm. "Come," he said, releasing my arm as we left the infirmary, indicating I should follow him.

Then he pointed to another larger, barrack-style building. "Where you eat. Later," he said. Then, pointing to himself, he added, "My name — Manoa."

"Aloha," I said. "Glad to meet you, Manoa." Not sure he understood me, I pointed to myself and said, "Dan."

He extended a stump with three fingers to shake hands; I hesitated only a moment. He smiled warmly, nodding as if he understood, then gestured for me to follow.

We walked to a large plot of earth, now being cleared. Someone else greeted me, handed me a hoe, and pointed to a section of earth. That was that.

I spent the rest of that day, until nightfall, working in the garden. Disorientating as it was, I felt glad to have a clear task to do — to be helping out — giving something for a change.

MANOA SHOWED ME where I'd sleep; at least I had my own room. I slept well and woke up hungry.

In the main dining hall, I sat across from some people who smiled at me but spoke mostly to one another in Hawaiian with a bit of pidgin English. Everyone at my table was friendly, handing me food again and again, while I tried to ignore their lesions.

That day, we — the gardening crew and I — made good progress, turning and breaking the soul, as rainsqualls passed over and were gone. I was careful to wear the sunscreen, and someone had loaned me a wide-brimmed hat.

The first few days were the hardest — the strangeness of being alone in this different world. The residents seemed to understand this. Another day passed in that garden. I was getting used to the routine.

Though nothing changed outwardly, something shifted inside me. As the people of this colony had come to accept their lives, I came to accept them, too, not as "lepers," but as people. I stopped being an observer and started to feel a sense of community.

After this, I was able to tune in to a special camaraderie here, born of isolation; from their own suffering came a deeper compassion for the pain of the world.

THE NEXT MORNING, returning from the latrine area, I saw an old man with twisted, deformed feet making his way across the compound, trembling as he leaned on a pair of crutches. Just then, one of the crutches broke and he fell. I ran over to help him up. He waved me off, muttering something and smiling a toothless smile, then stood up by himself. Holding the broken crutch in one hand, he hobbled on the other one off toward the infirmary.

There was no more work to be done in the garden until the seed arrived, but I was able to find plenty to do — in fact, I was busy morning till night, carrying water, helping change bandages. Someone even asked me to cut his hair, which I botched, but he didn't seem to mind at all.

All the while we chattered and laughed, only half understanding each other. These were among the most satisfying days I'd ever spent — lending a helping hand. And on the fifth day a wave of compassion washed over me — like nothing I had experienced before. Ever. And I understood Mama Chia's purpose. On that day I stopped worrying about getting "tainted" by the disease, and started wanting, really wanting, to be of service, in any way I could.

My heart was opening. I searched for something more I could contribute. I couldn't teach gymnastics; most of them were too old. I didn't have any other special skills that I knew of. Then, as I walked past a peaceful area just off the central compound, it came to me: I'd help make a pond. That was it! Something of beauty I could leave behind.

I'd worked for a landscape gardener one summer and had learned the basics. I found out that the community had some bags of concrete stored in a shed and all the tools we'd need. A picture formed in my mind: the vision of a beautiful, serene pond, a place to sit and meditate, or just take a brief rest. The ocean was just a few hundred yards away, but this pond would be special.

I showed a sketch to Manoa; he showed it to some of the others. They agreed it was a good idea, and a few men and I began digging.

THE NEXT DAY, just when we were ready to mix the concrete, Mama Chia showed up. "Well, Dan," she said, "a week has passed. I hope you've stayed out of mischief."

"It hasn't been a week already, has it? "

"Yes. One week."

"Well, you see... look, we're right in the middle of a project — can you come back in a few days?"

"I don't know," she said shaking her head. "We have other things to do — your training..."

"Yes I know, but I'd really like to finish this."

Mama Chia sighed and shrugged her shoulders. "Then we may not have time for a special technique to get in touch with — "

"Just a few more days!"

"Have it your way," she said, turning toward one of the bungalows. I caught a glimpse of her face. She looked positively smug. I only gave it a moment's reflection before lifting another bag of concrete.

MAMA CHIA RETURNED just in time to see us complete the stone-work. And the moment it was done, I knew it was time to leave. Several men came up to shake my hand. We'd formed a bond based on working on a common goal, sweating together — a bond men must have experienced for thousands of years. It felt good.

I was going to miss them all. I felt even closer to these outcasts from society than to my professional colleagues back in Ohio. Maybe because I had always felt like an outcast, too. Or maybe it was because of our shared task, or their openness, directness, and honesty. These men had nothing left to hide. They weren't trying to look good or save face. They had dropped their social masks, allowing me to drop mine, too.

I was turning to leave with my well-rounded kahuna when Tia came over and hugged both of us. I hugged her tenderly, feeling her sorrow and courage, knowing that she would soon have to give up her baby.

As MAMA CHIA led me down toward the beach, other feelings surfaced, too: All the gratitude, sorrow, and love for Mama Chia I had set aside these past ten days flooded in. Facing her, I placed my hands on her shoulders and looked into her eyes.

"You've been so good to me," I told her. "I wish there were something more I could do for you...." I had to take a slow, deep breath to hold off my sorrow. "You're such a ... kind person ... it just doesn't seem fair, and ... I don't deserve all the time, the energy, the life you've given me. How can I ever repay you?"

In answer, she hugged me for a long time. I held this old woman in a way I'd never been able to embrace Socrates.

Stepping back, she flashed me a bright smile: "I *love* what I do — someday you will understand this. And what I do is not for you, nor for Socrates, so thanks aren't necessary or appropriate. I act for a larger cause, a higher mission. By assisting you, I'll be assisting many others through you. Come," she said. "Let's go for a walk on the beach."

I surveyed the village, now back to its normal routine, and I felt inspired by the aloha spirit of these people. I saw them with different eyes than those I had come with. Even though other memories might fade, this would remain one of the most vivid — more real, and lasting, than any vision.

CHAPTER 18

Illuminations
in the Dead of Night

The seed of God is in us:
Pear seeds grow into pear trees;
Hazel seeds into hazel trees;
And God seeds into God.

— Meister Eckehart

NEITHER OF US SAID MUCH as we walked along the stretch of white sand; we just listened to the rush of waves, and the shrill cries of the albatross, patrolling the coast. Mama Chia scanned the horizon, watching the long shadows cast by the late afternoon sun like a cat, seeing things not visible to most of us. I examined the driftwood, pushed far up onto the beach by an unusually high tide, generated by a storm the night before. I combed the beach, looking for shells. Sachi wouldn't be impressed by shells, but Holly would like them. My little daughter, I thought, picturing Holly's sweet face, and missing her. I thought of Linda, too, and wondered if perhaps our lives were meant to go separate ways.

Glancing back, I saw the shadows cut across our meandering trail of footprints in the wet sand. I gazed down, searching for souvenirs from the sea, and Mama Chia continued to scan the horizon, and the stretch of beach ahead.

We sloshed out into knee-deep surf to go around a rocky point. She took a deep breath and I thought she was going to tell me something. But Mama Chia was reacting to one of the saddest and strangest sights I'd ever beheld: *Thousands* of starfish, washed up by the recent storm, littered the beach. Beautiful five-pointed stars, pink and tan, lay in the hot sand, drying out and dying.

I stopped in my tracks, awestruck by this massive marine graveyard. I'd read about grounded whales and dolphins, but I had never actually seen one. Now, confronted by thousands of dying creatures, I felt numb and helpless.

But without missing a single limping step, Mama Chia walked over to a nearby starfish, bent over to pick it up, walked to the water's edge, and placed it in the water. She then walked back and picked up another little star, and returned the creature to the sea.

Completely overwhelmed by the sheer number of starfish, I said, "Mama Chia, there are so many — how can what you're doing make any difference?"

She looked up at me for a moment as she lowered another starfish into the sea. "It makes a difference to this one," she replied.

Of course she was right. I picked up a starfish in each hand, and followed her example. Then I delivered another two into the sea. We continued through the afternoon and into the evening, under the light of the moon. Many starfish died anyway. But we did our best.

Mama Chia kept bending down, again and again and again. But there was nothing I could say to dissuade her. She would live until she died. And as long as I was here, on the island, I would help her. We worked long into the night. Finally, bone weary but feeling good, we lay in the soft sand, and slept.

I AWOKE AND SAT UP ABRUPTLY, thinking it was dawn. But the light that flickered in my eyes was a crackling fire, with Mama Chia sitting nearby, her back to me.

"Couldn't sleep?" I said as I approached, so as not to startle her.

"Had enough sleep," she said, never taking her eyes from the fire.

I stood behind her and massaged her shoulders and back. "What do you see in the fire?" I asked, without expecting a reply.

"What if I told you I wasn't from this planet?" she asked.

"What?"

"Suppose I told you that neither was Socrates? Or you?"

I didn't know what to say — whether to take her seriously. "Is that what you saw in the fire?" was all I could think to ask.

"Sit down," she said. "See for yourself."

I sat, and gazed into the dancing flames.

Mama Chia rose slowly, and began to knead the muscles of my back with her strong hands. "You asked me why I've been here for you. It's because we're family," she revealed. "Part of the same spiritual family."

"What do you mean — " I never got to finish my sentence. Mama Chia gave me a solid whack at the back of my neck. I saw stars, then only the fire . . . deeper . . . deeper . . .

I SAW THE BEGINNINGS of time and space, when Spirit became the "ten thousand things": the star forms, the planets, the mountains, the seas, and the creatures great and small that spawned there.

But there were no humans. Before history, in a time of magic, when Mind allowed it, the legends were born. The animals evolved on earth, growing from all that preceded them. But no human souls existed on the planet.

I saw a vision of the ancient universe, where, within the curves of space, angelic souls played in realms of freedom and bliss. This memory, stored within the most ancient records of the psyche, became the archetype for that place we call heaven.

A wave of these souls came down to earth because they were curious about the material realm — about the animal forms, and about sexual-creative energy — about what it would be like in a body.

And so, they overshadowed the primitive forms of animals that roamed the earth; they entered them, saw through their eyes, felt through their skin, and experienced the material realm and life on earth.

I saw them, I felt them, as they grew ready to leave their animal hosts, and return to their Source. But these souls misjudged the magnetic attraction of the material realm; they became trapped, identified with the animal consciousness. Thus began a great adventure on this planet.

These soul energies, and their humanlike higher consciousness within the animals, impacted the DNA structure, causing immediate and radical evolutionary leaps. This was revealed to me in visions within the genetic spirals themselves.

The next generation of creatures provided the basis for the Greek myths — centaurs, mermaids, satyrs, and nymphs; half animal, half human, they were the source of legends, the Olympian gods cohabitating with animals and humans.

The first wave had forgotten that they were of Spirit, not of flesh; they had become identified with their hosts. So a wave of missionary souls came down to rescue the first wave, to pull them out. But they, too, were trapped.

Time flashed by, centuries in an instant. A second rescue mission was sent; this time, only the most powerful souls made the attempt — and very few escaped. They, too, remained, trapped by their own desire for power. They became the kings, the queens, the pharaohs, and the chiefs — the rulers of the lands of earth. Some were like King Arthur; others, like Attila the Hun.

A third and final rescue mission was sent. These very special souls were the most courageous of all — the peaceful warrior souls — because they knew they weren't coming back; they knew they would be destined to live within a mortal body for aeons — suffering, losing loved ones, in mortal pain and fear, until all souls were free.

They were a volunteer mission. And they came to remind all others who they are. They include carpenters, students, doctors, artists, athletes, musicians, and ne'er-do-wells — geniuses and madmen, criminals and saints. Most have forgotten their mission, but an ember still glows within the hearts and memories of those who are destined to awaken to their heritage as the servants of humanity, and to awaken others.

These rescuers are not "better" souls, unless love makes them so. They may be lost, or found. But they are awakening, now. Hundreds of thousands of souls on the planet — becoming a spiritual family.

I PULLED MY EYES from the flames and turned to Mama Chia, sitting next to me. Still gazing into the fire, she said, "My soul is one of those who came in the final rescue mission. As was the soul of the man you call 'Socrates.' And your soul as well...."

That explained that sense of recognition I had felt in meeting her — and a few others in my life as well.

"There are many others," she continued, "hundreds of thousands, scattered across the planet — who feel a call to serve; who know deep inside that they are here to do something, but cannot quite articulate what that something may be. More coming in all the time, many of our children, searching to find out who they are and what they are here to do. All have in common a certain rest-lessness — a deep sense of being somehow *different,* of being odd-balls, visitors here, never quite fitting in. We feel at times a longing to 'go home,' but we're not exactly sure where that is. We often have giving, but rather insecure natures.

"Well, we are not here to 'fit in,' as much as we might like to. We are here to teach, to lead, to heal, to remind others, if only by our example.

"The earth has been the school for most human souls, but our souls are not yet completely of this earth. We have been schooled elsewhere; there are things we just know without knowing how we know — things we recognize, as if this is a refresher course, and we are most definitely here on a service mission.

"Your search, Dan, will be for ways to make a difference — first to awaken yourself, then to find the right leverage, the best means to find the calling most natural and effective in reaching out to others. It is like this for all the peaceful warriors who share this mission. One of us might become a haircutter; another, a teacher; a third, a stockbroker or pet groomer or counselor. Some of us become famous; others remain anonymous. Each of us plays a part."

We sat there, staring out to sea for a while — I don't know how long — before she spoke again. "So here you are, one of many like-minded souls in a very different 'wrapping,' treading water in the ocean of karma, but there's a rowboat nearby — much closer to you than to many others. Before you can help oth-ers into the boat, you have to get in yourself.

"And that is what your preparation is about. That is why you met Socrates, and why I am here working with you. Not because you are somehow special or more deserving, but because you have within you that unstoppable impulse to share yourself with others." She paused. "Someday, you will write, teach, and do other things, too, to reach out to your spiritual family, to remind them of their mission, to give the clarion call."

The weight of responsibility hit me like a falling safe. "Teach these things? I can't even remember half of what you say. And I've no talent for writing," I protested. "My grades in English weren't so good."

She smiled. "I see what I see."

In another few hours, it would be dawn; the fire had died down to embers when I spoke again. "You say there are many souls like me — "

"Yes, but you combine a particular set of talents and qualities that make you a good transmitter. So you and Socrates found each other, and he sent you to me."

Mama Chia then lay down, curled up, and slept. I stared out to sea until the first hint of the sun lit the sky at the eastern tip of the island, and sleep finally came.

MORNING. Strange, waking up on a beach, the warm tropical air my only blanket. Here the air felt comfortable even at dawn, like a summer morning in the Midwest.

Sleeping in the open air whetted my appetite, and breakfast, courtesy of Mama Chia's bottomless backpack, was both simple and memorable: a handful of figs, a few macadamia nuts, an orange, and a banana. An illuminating night had passed; I wondered what the new day would bring.

As it turned out, the day was uneventful. We spent most of it hiking home, and the evening having tea and listening to music on her old phonograph. Mama Chia retired early; I slept on her living room floor.

The following day, I would meet a ghost, and set into motion a series of events that would again change the course of my life.

CHAPTER 19

Revelation and the Warrior's Way

Take time to deliberate,
but when the time for action arrives,
stop thinking and go in.

— Andrew Jackson

IT CAME OUT OF NOWHERE, on an ordinary day, as surprises do. It came from seeds planted in the past. "I thought you might like to meet Sachi's family," Mama Chia said as we walked along an unfamiliar path into the forest. Why was she smiling like a Cheshire cat?

Half a mile later, we entered a clearing where a lovely house stood, larger than Mama Chia's but similar in design, with a garden to the side.

A little boy, about five years old, emerged, jumped down the two steps, and ran straight at me, down the path. With a "Hi, Dan!" he jumped up into my arms, laughing, as if he'd known me all my life.

"Well, hi..."

"My name's Socrates," he said proudly.

"Really?" I said, surprised. "Well, that's a fine name." I looked up to see a small, slim woman, very lovely, wrapped in a deep blue, flowered sarong, following her son. But she had no intention, it turned out, of jumping into my arms.

Smiling graciously, she held out her hand. "Hello, Dan, I'm Sarah."

"Hello, I'm . . . glad to meet you." Puzzled, I glanced at Mama Chia. "Does everyone around here know me?" I asked.

Mama Chia, Sarah, Sachi, and little Socrates all laughed with delight; I didn't understand what was so funny, but they were certainly enjoying something.

"Sachi and Soc's father has told them a lot about you," Mama Chia said, pointing behind me.

I turned, "Well, who — ?"

"Hello, Dan," a voice interrupted me.

I turned and stared, then gaped, my jaw open wide. I had never seen a ghost before. But there he was — tall and slim, with a curly blond beard, deep-set eyes, and a crinkled smile. "Joseph? Is that really you?"

He gave me a bear hug and slapped me on the back. Then I stepped away. "But . . . but he told me you died — of leukemia . . ."

"Died?" said Joseph, still grinning. "Well, I *am* a little tired . . ."

"What happened?" I asked. "How — "

"Why don't you two go for a walk?" Sarah suggested. "You have some catching up to do."

"Good idea," Joseph answered.

As we walked slowly into the forest, Joseph cleared up the mystery of his apparent death.

"I did have leukemia," he confirmed. "I still do, but with Mama Chia's help, my body is handling it okay. But in a way, Socrates was right. I did die to the world for several months. I became a renunciate, a hermit. I told him I was going to disappear into the forest, fast, and pray until I died or healed. Come to think of it," he said, "I'd better go back a few years to fill you in.

"I was raised in the Midwest by a family of strangers. I'll always be grateful to them for getting me through my childhood diseases — all those nights I kept them up — and for giving me food and shelter. But I never quite fit in, you know? It was as if they had adopted me, found me somewhere."

"Yes," I said. "I know."

"So the first chance I got, I hit the road — worked my way across the country, headed out toward the West Coast, doing odd jobs, mostly. And when I got to L.A., I just kept going. I ended up here, on Molokai. I had a friend who lived here. He encouraged me to settle. So I became a young 'agricultural entrepreneur,' and cultivated cannabis — "

"You grew marijuana?"

"Yes. That was 1960, and it just seemed like the thing to do. I don't do that anymore, because — well, now it just doesn't seem like the thing to do. I still cook when I get a chance, but there aren't many chances around here. So I build cabinets and bureaus — that sort of thing. I like working with wood. It pays the bills and keeps me out of mischief." He smiled.

"Anyway, back then, I made a lot of money, and about that time, I married Sarah. In 1964, Sachi was born, and..." Joseph paused here — I think it pained him to recall it — "I just split. I..." He searched for the right words. "Dan, you understand about the three selves, right?"

I nodded. "I am acquainted with my Basic Self, but I sort of lost touch with my Higher Self," I answered.

"Just the opposite with me," said Joseph. "I rejected my Basic Self. All I wanted was to be up and out of here — to go home, wherever that was. I tried everything to get high. I couldn't cope with the hassles of daily life. I told myself I was a 'spiritual being,' a 'creative artist' who didn't have to deal with 'reality.' I spent most of my time meditating, communing with nature, reading — all the time hoping to go 'somewhere else' — anywhere I wouldn't have to deal with the drudgery, the details, the physicality of this realm.

"Then, when Sachi came along — I wasn't ready to have children, to work on a relationship or responsibilities; I didn't know how to deal with it. So I took half our funds and split. I didn't know where to go, but I ended up in Berkeley, California, and after a few weeks, I ran into this old guy — "

"At a gas station," I laughed, completing Joseph's sentence for him.

"You can imagine the rest. Socrates insisted I get responsible work before he'd teach me, so I started the café. We made a deal," he said. "I fed him some good food, and he turned my life upside down."

"Sounds fair to me." I said, grinning.

"More than fair," Joseph agreed. "I got my money's worth; he really kicked my ass. I haven't seen him for about five years, though. Went back to visit two years ago, but he'd gone. He once said something about going to the mountains, maybe somewhere in the Sierras — I don't know. I doubt we'll see him for a while."

"Well, how did you turn it around? I mean, you came back here, made a go of your relationship — you build cabinets, maintain a business..."

Joseph smiled at me as I counted all the responsible things he did on my fingers. "It still isn't easy," he said. "But do you remember what Soc used to remind us? You know, about a chain breaking at its weakest link — and so do we? Well, I just decided I'd better work on my weak links."

"I still have my work cut out for me," I said. "But I'm really not sure how to 'work on' getting into my heart. Mama Chia said it had to come of its own accord."

Joseph paused, thoughtful, and said, "I think it's just a matter of becoming more and more aware. Simple awareness can set in motion many kinds of healing."

We sat quietly for a while, then I reminded him, "You said you were ill."

Startled out of reverie, Joseph replied, "Yes — and I had intended to go to the mountains to fast and pray, as I told you. But then I remembered something Socrates had told me about life being hard either way, whether you space out and give up, or whether you go for it. Well, it sank in. I realized that the mountain hermit thing would be another way to get out of the body, to escape. I probably would have died.

"But I decided to return to Molokai, come what may, to take up where I'd left off — but do it right — with as much time as I had left to do it in, if Sarah would have me back.

"She welcomed me with open arms," he said. "Everything worked out so incredibly," he said. "As soon as I committed to coming back and digging in and going for it, it all fell into place."

"How?"

"Well, that's when I started working with Mama Chia. She taught me a few things, and helped me to heal."

"It sure worked," I said. "I've seen your family."

Joseph gave me a look of complete contentment — a look I envied. And I reflected sadly about the shambles in which I'd left my own marriage and family. But that was going to change, I told myself.

Joseph stood slowly. "I'm glad to see you again, Dan."

"Best thing that's happened to me in a long time," I replied. "And a lot of good things have happened."

"I believe that," he said.

"Amazing how we both found our way to Mama Chia."

"It sure is," he echoed. "And so is she."

"Hey, and speaking of amazing, that daughter of yours is a wonder," I said — then I remembered what had happened in town. "She did get a bit of a scare, though."

"I know...Sachi told me about it. But from what I hear, she wasn't the one who was in trouble."

"You got that right," I declared. "But that incident taught me something: I need to learn some martial arts."

"I'm surprised Socrates never taught you. He was pretty amazing at it, you know."

"Yeah, I know. But I was so focused on gymnastics — you remember."

"Oh, that's right." Joseph looked thoughtful, then said, "Well, Fuji used to study some kind of karate. He's a good man. Maybe he can help you, but, Dan, for this situation, I don't think learning to fight is really the answer. I know those boys. They're not really bad kids. Once they helped me push my car half a mile to a gas station. They're just bored, and frustrated. There aren't many jobs; they probably don't feel terribly good about themselves — same old story." He sighed.

"Yeah, I know," I replied. I looked at Joseph. "I'm glad you're alive."

"Me, too," he answered.

As WE EMERGED from the forest and approached Joseph's front steps, little Socrates came running, jumped up into Joseph's arms, then turned his dad's face so they were nose to nose. It was clear he wanted his father's undivided attention.

Joseph kissed Soc on the nose and turned to me. "I'm going

back to Oahu tomorrow to complete a job, and, well — I need to spend some time with my family."

"Oh — sure," I said. "Maybe I'll see you when you get back."

"Count on it," he smiled. Sarah came out, too, and put her arm around her husband. They waved as I turned back down the path. I heard Sachiko's voice from their cabin as she called to her family, "Food's ready."

Walking back to my cabin, I felt a stab of regret as I thought of Linda and Holly. I wondered if I'd ever have a happy family of my own.

THAT AFTERNOON, wandering through the forest paths, I found my way to Sei Fujimoto's house. Mitsu answered the door. "I just put the baby down," she whispered. "Fuji's not here, but he should be back any time. You want to wait inside?"

"Thanks, Mrs. Fujimoto — "

"Call me Mitsu."

"Thanks, Mitsu, but I'd like to wait in the garden for a while, if that's okay."

"Play with the garden spirits, eh?" she said, smiling.

"Something like that," I replied.

I had always had a special feeling about gardens, about sitting in the dirt, surrounded by plants. So I lay on my side, feeling the warm, rich earth radiate pleasant heat on my chest and stomach, and I gazed up close at a squash blossom, its yellow flower so delicate, with the most subtle fragrance, waving in the gentle breeze.

And I did feel the garden spirits — a distinctive energy so different from the cold, functional concrete of the cities and sidewalks, expanses of stark gray blocks, with their stiffness and rigidity. Here, I felt at peace. . . .

The honk of Fuji's truck brought me back to the business at

hand. I walked over to him, waved, and helped him unload some bags of fertilizer to complement his compost pile. "Nice to see you, Dan — glad to have some help."

"Actually, Fuji, I came to ask for *your* help," I said.

He stopped and looked over at me, curious. "How can I help you?"

"Joseph said you used to know some karate."

A smile of recognition passed over his face. "Oh, I see. Yes, I've studied a little of this, a little of that. I'm not as quick now — have to hit the bad guys with bags of fertilizer, or with my car," he joked. "What do you want with karate — somebody you want me to beat up?" His smile broadened as he struck a pose, puffing up his chest in mock bravado.

"No," I laughed. "Nothing like that. It's just that I think I should learn how to defend myself."

"Not a bad idea; you never know when you'll need it," he said. "There's a pretty good school in town — I've stopped by and watched a few times."

"Oh, I don't think I'd be able to take lessons in town right now; I don't have the time."

"What you want to do, take a self-defense pill?" he asked.

"No," I answered, laughing again.

"I was wondering if you could teach me something."

"Me?" He shook his head. "It's been too many years, Dan. I've forgotten more than I know." He took a stance, kicked the air, then held his back, comically. "See what I mean?"

"Fuji, I'm serious. This is important to me."

He hesitated. "I'd like to help you, Dan, but you better study with a real teacher. Besides, I've got to run up to the ranch and mend some fence."

"Well, I've got nothing else to do; how about if I help you with the fence?"

"Okay. Then at least I can teach you the fine art of fencing," he punned. "I'll tell Mitsu we're going."

"And think about the other lessons, too, okay?"

He called back to me: "I don't like to think too much about anything."

WE SPENT THE REST OF THE DAY mending fences. It was hard work — digging postholes, pounding the uprights, sawing and chopping. Fuji loaned me a pair of his gloves or my hands would have blistered; it reminded me of the old gymnastic days. Mitsu invited me for a vegetarian dinner of steaming rice, vegetables, and tofu. Then the baby's cry was Mitsu's signal to say good night.

"You did a good job, today, Dan," Fuji said, handing me a ten dollar bill — the first money I'd earned in a while.

"I can't take your money, Fuji."

"Not my money — yours. I don't work for free; neither do you," he insisted, pressing it into my hand.

"Well, then, maybe I can use it to pay you for a martial art lesson."

Fuji knit his brows in thought before answering. "I could give you one painting lesson, but that wouldn't make you a painter."

"Sure it would." I said. "Just not a very good one."

Scratching his head as if the idea pained him, Fuji said, "Let me think about it."

"Good enough, and good night."

THE NEXT MORNING, Fuji woke me. "Okay," he said. "I can show you one or two things." I opened my eyes to see him standing over me. "I'll wait outside," he said.

Jumping out of bed, I made a quick pit stop, then emerged from the cabin with shorts on and shirt in hand.

I followed him to a spot of level ground about twenty feet from the cabin, where he turned, and said, "Stand here. Face me."

"Uh, shouldn't we warm up or something?" I asked, accustomed to my old gymnastic habits.

"Don't need a warm-up in Hawaii," he said. "Hawaii *is* a warm-up. Besides, no warm-up required for what we do; we get warmer as we go. Okay?"

"Okay; now I'm gonna show you a very good martial arts movement." Taking a comfortable stance, he said, "Copy me." He let both arms drop to his sides, then began to bend his right arm at the elbow, raising his hand. I did the same. Then he extended his hand forward, toward me. I mirrored each movement as precisely as I could. As I did this, he reached out with that hand and started shaking mine. "How do you do," he said, grinning, "nice to meet you, let's be friends, okay?"

"Fuji," I said, letting go of his hand. "Quit playing around; I'm serious!"

"Me, too," he assured me. "This is one of my favorite techniques. It's called 'making friends.' I always teach it first."

"Then there's more?" I asked, hopeful.

"Sure, but if the first technique works, you don't need any others. I also have a move called 'handing wallet to thief.' Sometimes avoids pain."

"Fuji, if those bully boys in town ever run into me again, I may not be able to shake hands, and they don't want my wallet; they want my head."

"Okay," he said, serious this time. "I better show you a few things."

"Kicks and punches?"

"No — they hurt people."

Getting frustrated, I asked, "What kind of martial artist are you, anyway?"

"Pacifist kind," he replied. "You hurt other people enough times, you get tired of seeing blood. Anyway, I can help you with self-*defense,* not offense."

FOR THE NEXT SEVERAL HOURS, he proceeded to show me a series of evasive maneuvers, twists, and turns, and ways to shield myself with circular movements of my arms — simple, and elegant. "I like to keep it simple," he said. "Easier to practice."

He told me to visualize actual attackers, larger and meaner than I would ever be likely to meet. Soon, the defensive elements took on a life of their own.

I reached into my pocket and offered him back his ten dollars.

"No," he waved me off. "This wasn't a lesson — this was play. Brought back some good memories. Keep your money — may come in handy."

"Thank you, Fuji."

"Thank you, too, Dan."

We shook hands. "Still my favorite move, that one," he said.

"Fuji," I asked as I walked with him back to his cabin, "did a spry old man with white hair, a friend of Mama Chia's, ever visit around here? His name is Socrates."

Fuji knit his brows, then a smile came to his face. "Yes, I think so — once, some years ago — short white hair, wearing the brightest Hawaiian shirt I ever saw. Must have come from California," he added with a grin. "Very interesting man."

I could just imagine Socrates in a Hawaiian shirt. I wondered if I would ever see my old teacher and friend again, and all at once I missed him terribly.

The Great Leap

Anything can be achieved in small, deliberate steps.

But there are times you need the courage to take a great leap.

You can't cross a chasm in two small jumps.

— David Lloyd George

CHAPTER 20

Odyssey

The secret of success in life:
Prepare for opportunity when it comes.

— Benjamin Disraeli

As WE NEARED FUJI'S HOUSE, the stars were just coming out, and the moon was nearly full. Except for the crickets, and a soft wind, the silent forest was asleep.

"You sure you won't stay for dinner?" he asked. "Mitsu is always happy to set out one more plate."

"No, really, I have some things to do," I said, but the truth was, with the baby and all, I didn't want to impose. Fuji stopped and stared into space. He looked serious.

Just then, I had a kind of premonition — not bad, exactly, but unsettling.

"What is it, Fuji? Do you feel something, too?"

"Yes," he said.

"What could it — " My thoughts naturally drifted to Mama Chia. "Mama Chia?" I said. "Do you think — "

Fuji looked at me. "I'll drop by — just in case."

"I'll go with you," I said.

"No," he replied. "It may be nothing."

"I want to go."

Fuji hesitated, then said, "Okay." We walked quickly up the path toward her house.

The feeling of foreboding grew stronger for both of us as we drew near her house. "It's probably nothing," I said, trying to convince myself that everything was all right.

WE WERE ABOUT TO GO INSIDE when Fuji spotted her, slumped against a tree adjacent to the garden. She looked so peaceful there, so still, with the moonlight shining on her closed eyes. Fuji rushed to her side and started to check her pulse.

In shock, I knelt slowly down next to him and stroked her silver hair. My eyes filled with tears. "I wanted to thank you, Mama Chia," I said. "I wanted to say good — "

We jumped back in surprise as Mama Chia sat up quickly and yelled, "Can't a woman take a nap under the stars anymore?"

Fuji and I looked at each other, delighted. "We thought you — you — " I stammered.

"I was checking your pulse — " Fuji fared no better.

Then she realized what we had assumed. "You thought I'd kicked the bucket, did you? Well, don't worry, I was just practicing. I want to get it right. We may have to rehearse every day until you two can stop acting like bumbling fools," she said, laughing.

A delighted Fuji excused himself; dinner was waiting. But before he left, he stopped to give me some good advice. "Dan, about those boys in town — "

"Yes?" I asked.

"Sometimes, the best way to win a fight is to lose it."

"What do you mean?"

"Think about it," he said, then he turned and headed home for Mitsu's vegetarian stew.

THAT NIGHT, in Mama Chia's living room, she and I toasted each other's health with several glasses of sake. My system was so clean from the exercise and simple diet that the sake's effect was devastating — which is to say I got even more maudlin than usual. With moist eyes, I swore everlasting devotion to Mama Chia, and said good-bye to her "forever, just in case." She patted my hand indulgently, smiled, and remained silent.

At some point, I must have fallen asleep on the floor, because that's where I found myself the next morning, my ears ringing like the bells of Notre Dame. I wanted desperately to distance myself from my throbbing head, but there was nowhere to run.

Mama Chia got up looking obnoxiously chipper and made me one of her "special remedies — worse than death itself."

"Speaking of death," I said, each word sending stabbing pains through me, "I don't think you're the one who's going to die soon — it's me, I can tell — and I hope it's real soon," I added, rolling my eyes. "Oh, I feel sick."

"Stop rolling your eyes," she suggested. "That will help."

"Thanks. I didn't know I was rolling them."

An hour later, I felt much better, much clearer, and with that clarity came a new wave of concern.

"You know, you really scared me last night. I just stood there. I felt helpless — like there was nothing I could do."

Mama Chia sat on a cushion on the floor and looked at me. "Let's get this straight once and for all, Dan. There is nothing you're supposed to do. If you want peace of mind, I suggest you resign as general manager of the universe.

"I'm telling you, Dan, it's homestretch for me — whatever you do or don't do. Maybe tomorrow, maybe a few months — but soon. I'm packed and ready to go," she said, putting her feet on the edge of the couch and gazing up at the ceiling.

"Mama Chia," I confessed, "when I first came here, I believed I needed you only to tell me where to go next."

She smiled at this.

"But now, I don't know what I could learn that you and Socrates haven't already taught me."

She looked at me. "There's always more to learn; one thing prepares you for the next."

"That place in Asia — where you met Socrates — is that where I'm to go next?"

She offered no response.

"What is it — don't you trust me enough to tell me?"

"These are all fair questions, Dan, and I understand how you feel. But I can't simply hand you a name and address."

"Why not?"

Mama Chia took a breath as she considered how to respond. "Call it the House Rules," she said. "Or call it a safety device, an initiation. Only those sensitive enough, open enough, are meant to find it."

"Socrates was about as helpful as you in terms of specifics. He told me that if I couldn't find my way to you, I wasn't ready."

"So you understand."

"Yes, but that doesn't mean I like it."

"Like it or not, there's a bigger picture here," she reminded me. "And more people are involved than just you and me and Socrates. We are only a few interwoven threads in a larger quilt. And there are mysteries I don't even try to fathom; I just enjoy them."

"Socrates once gave me a business card," I told her. "It's at home for safekeeping. Below his name, it says, 'Paradox, Humor, and Change.'"

Smiling, Mama Chia said, "That's life, all right. Socrates always did have a way of cutting to the heart of things." Then she touched my arm, and said, "So you see, it's not a matter of whether or not I trust you, Dan. It's more a matter of you trusting yourself."

"I'm not sure what you mean."

"Then trust that, too."

"But I remember Socrates saying you would show me the way."

"Yes, *show* you the way — not send you a telegram. To find the hidden schools, you have to discover the Inner Records. The House Rules don't permit me to tell you directly; I can only train you to see, to help prepare you. The map is inside."

"Inside? Where?"

"The hidden schools are often in the middle of a city, or in a small village — maybe right next door to where you live — not invisible at all. But most people walk right past — too busy visiting the caves in Nepal and Tibet, searching where they expect to find holiness. Until we warriors explore the caves and shadow places within our own minds, we see only our own reflections — and the masters sound like fools, because only fools are listening.

"Now," she continued, "is the time when the invisible becomes visible again, and angels take wing. You are one of these. It has been my duty, my happy duty, to help you along. Like Socrates, I'm a cheerleader to the soul," she said. "We're here to support you, not make it easy for you.

"*You* have to find the path ahead, as you found me. All I can do is point in the right direction, push you onward, and wish you Godspeed."

She saw my expression. "Relax your brows, Dan. And stop trying to figure everything out. You don't have to know everything about the ocean to swim in it."

"Do you think I'm ready to move on?"

"No, not yet. If you left now — " She left the sentence unfinished, and changed course. "You're almost there — maybe an hour from now, or a few years. I hope to remain here long enough to see you — "

"Make the leap," I finished for her.

"Yes. Because, as I've said, after the fourth floor, it's an express elevator."

"I'd make the leap today, right now, if I knew how," I said, frustrated. "I'd do anything for you; just tell me what to do."

"I wish it were that simple — to just tell you. But change has to come from inside you — like a flower from its seed — you can't rush it. We don't control the timetable.

"In the meantime, just do what feels right; deal with whatever stands in front of you. Use everything to grow, to uplift. Take care of any unfinished business on the lower floors. Face your fears; do whatever you have to do to maximize your health and energy. Channel and discipline that energy; you have to master yourself before you can go beyond that self."

She paused, and took another deep breath before saying, "I've shown you what you need to know. It will help you, or not, depending on what you do with it."

Heavyhearted, I stared at the floor, and said in a hushed tone, almost to myself, "I keep losing teachers. First Socrates sends me away, and now you tell me you'll be leaving soon."

"You don't ever want to get too attached to any one teacher," she said. "Don't mistake the wrapping for the gift. Do you understand?"

"I think I do," I replied. "It means I have another wild-goose chase in store — looking for someone without a face in a place with no name."

She smiled. "When the student is ready, the teacher appears."

"I've heard that one before," I said.

"But do you really understand? That statement really means 'When the student is ready, the teacher appears — *everywhere*': in the sky, in the trees, in taxicabs and banks, in therapists' offices and service stations, in your friends and in your enemies. We're all teachers for one another. There are teachers in every neighborhood, in every city, state, and country — teachers for every level of consciousness. As in every field, some are more skilled or aware than others. But it doesn't matter. Because everything is an oracle; it's all connected; every piece mirrors the Whole, when you have eyes to see, and ears to hear. This may sound abstract to you now, but one day — and that day may not be too far away — you will absolutely understand it. And when you do," she said, picking up a shiny stone, "you'll be able to gaze into this stone, or examine the veins on this leaf, or watch a paper cup blowing in the wind, and you'll understand the hidden principles of the universe."

After pondering this, I asked, "Is there something wrong with human teachers?"

"Of course there is! Because every teacher in a human body is going to have some kind of imbalance, eccentricity, or weakness. Maybe the problems are big, and maybe little. Maybe it's sex or food or power — or worse, the teacher may go and die on you." She paused here, for effect.

"But for most people," she continued, "a human teacher is the best game in town — a living example, a mirror. It's easier to understand a human's writing or speaking than the language of the clouds or cats or a shaft of lightning in a purple sky.

"Humans, too, have their wisdom to share, but human teachers come and go; once you open the Inner Records, you see it all directly, from the inside, and the Universal Teacher appears."

"What can I do now to prepare myself?" I asked.

Mama Chia paused, grew very quiet, and stared at nothing. Then she turned to me. "I've done what I can to help you prepare."

"Prepare for what?" I asked.

"For what's to come."

"I've never liked riddles."

"Maybe that's why life has given you so many." She smiled.

"How do I know I'm ready?"

"You could know by faith," she said. "But your faith in yourself isn't strong enough. So you need a challenge — a test — to mirror and prove what you have, or haven't, yet learned."

Mama Chia stood, and began pacing across the room, then gazing out the window, then pacing some more. Finally, she stopped, and said to me, "There is a treasure on this island — well hidden from unprepared eyes. I want you to find it. If you do, then you're ready to leave, and go on with my blessings. If not —" She didn't complete the sentence except to say, "Meet me at sunset, tonight, in the forest; I'll explain everything to you then."

Redbird landed on the windowsill outside. Watching him, I said, "I'll be there. Where exactly shall we meet?" When I looked up, she was gone. "Mama Chia?" I called. *"Mama Chia?"* No answer. I searched the house and out in back, but I knew I wouldn't find her, until sunset. But where? And how? That, I sensed, was to be my first task.

I RESTED MOST OF THE AFTERNOON — no telling what I'd have to do after the sun went down. I lay on my bed, too excited to sleep. A part of me kept sorting through the files of everything I'd learned about the three selves and the seven floors of the tower of life; images and feelings kept floating by.

I couldn't even remember how the world looked before I met Mama Chia. I wondered how I saw anything at all. But visions were one thing; real-world tests were another. What did she have in store?

I thought of all the likely, and unlikely, places she would wait, but I soon concluded that trying to figure it out would be fruitless.

Then I thought, Basic Selves are in contact, so my Basic Self should know where hers is. I only had to pay attention to its messages through my intuitive sense, my gut feelings. I could home in on her like a Geiger counter! Now I knew how — but could I actually do it?

I knew I'd have to relax my body and clear my Conscious Self in order to sense the messages from my Basic Self. So, in the late afternoon, I found a mound of dirt at the edge of the forest and sat in meditation. Letting my breath rise and fall of its own accord, I let my thoughts, sensations, and emotions rise and fall like waves on the sea. Unperturbed by the currents of the mind, I watched them come, and let them go, without clinging or attachment.

Just before sunset, I rose, stretched, took a few deep breaths, breathing out any tension, concern, or anxiety that might interfere — and strode to the center of the clearing. Stay confident, I reminded myself. Trust the Basic Self; it knows.

First I tried to visualize where she was. I relaxed, and waited for an image. Her face appeared, but it felt like a picture I had constructed from memory, and I couldn't really see her surroundings. Then I listened with my inner ears for some kind of clue, maybe even her voice. But that didn't work either.

As a trained athlete, I had developed a refined kinesthetic sense, acutely aware of my body. So I used this sense, turning slowly in a circle, feeling for a direction. Then my mind intervened: She'll probably be sitting right on her front porch. No, she'll be at the frog pond. Maybe she's in the forest near Joseph and Sarah's, or Fuji and Mitsu's. Or she'll sneak into my cabin and wait for me to give up. Suddenly aware of what I was doing, I threw all that away. This was no time for logic or reason.

Feel it! I told myself. I silently asked my Basic Self to tell me. I waited, still turning slowly. Nothing, and then, "Yes!" In my excitement, I had shouted out loud. I pointed my arm, or it pointed itself — I don't know for certain — and felt an inner confirmation, like gut feelings I'd had in the past, only stronger. My Conscious Self jumped in with all kinds of doubts: This is silly — just your imagination. You can't know this, you're making it up.

Ignoring my thoughts, I followed my arm, up at an angle, to the left of the path toward the ridge. I started walking, and the feeling remained strong. I headed deeper into the forest, off the path, and stopped. I turned, feeling like a blind man, relying on new inner senses. She felt closer; then doubts assaulted me once again.

But the feeling was stronger than my doubts, and it told me she was near. I turned once again in a circle, stopped, and walked forward. Right into a tree. As I touched the tree, it said in a loud voice, "That was too easy; next time, I'll make you wear a blindfold."

"Mama Chia!" I cried, thrilled, stepping around the tree to see her sitting there. "I did it. It worked!" I was jumping up and down. "I didn't *know* where you were; I couldn't have known. But I found you."

This proved to me that there is more to this world, more to human beings, and more to me, than meets the eye. Actually trusting my Basic Self, and seeing how the Conscious Self could get in the way, brought all the concepts I had learned into focus, and into reality. "This is incredible!" I said. "What a magical world!"

With a considerable but gallant effort, I helped her to her feet and reached around her in a bear hug. "Thank you! That was really fun."

"Like any child, the Basic Self loves to have fun," she said. "That's why you feel so much energy."

I soon calmed, however, and told her, "I'll find this treasure, whatever it is, if that's the challenge you have for me. But I don't really have to look anywhere else; you're the treasure. I want to stay here, with you, as long as I can."

"Dan," she said, taking me gently by the shoulders, "this tells me you're close to making the leap, so very close. But I'm not the one you're here to serve. I'm just a way station. Remember me with gratitude, if you will. But not for me — for you — because gratitude opens the heart." In the last pink light of the sunset, her face looked beatific as she smiled at me, mirroring back all the love I felt for her.

"And now," she said, "the time has come for you to begin." She sat down once again, took her notepad and a pen out of her pack, and closed her eyes. As I watched her, she just sat and breathed, waiting. Then she began to write in her trembling hand — slowly at first, then faster. When she finished, she handed the note to me. It read:

Over water, under sea,
in the forest high you'll be.
Trust your instinct, in the sea;
bring the treasure home to me.

If you find it, as you might,
you will travel, day and night.
As you see it, you will know,
as above, then so below.
Once you grasp it, you will be
ready then to cross the sea.

I read the note a second time. "What does it mean?" I asked, looking up. She had disappeared again. "Damn it! How do you do that?" I yelled into the forest. Then, with a sigh, I sat down and wondered what to do next.

So, I was to go on a treasure hunt — some kind of odyssey. Well, I could start in the morning — that made sense. But the riddle said I would travel "day and night." On the other hand, there was no use starting until I knew where I was going. I looked at the riddle again. Clearly, I was to go a number of places: over water, under sea — that part had me baffled — and in the forests, too. Most puzzling was the last part: "As you see it, you will know, as above, then so below."

On an impulse, perhaps hoping for a sign or clue, I decided to hike up into the forest to get a better perspective. A full moon was rising in the east, low on the horizon, but enough to light my way.

"Walking alone in a forest at night playing hide-and-seek with the moon," I sang aloud, in time with my footsteps as I hiked rhythmically up the damp, moonlit path. I felt fresh, alert, and alive. The forest didn't really change much at night, but I did. Mysterious and unaccustomed activity brought my Basic Self to the surface. I enjoyed the excitement.

A warm glow began in my abdomen and, like an expanding energy, bubbled up through my chest so that I had to let out a cry like a bird. "Eeeaaahh," I screeched in a high-pitched tone. I felt like a bird, then like a mountain lion, padding silently through the night. I'd never had a challenge quite like this one.

As I climbed higher, a light sheen of sweat formed on my face and chest in the warm night. And I wondered about the mystery of this life. This magical night seemed unreal, or rather, as real as a dream. Maybe I *was* dreaming. Maybe I fell off that surfboard into the sea; perhaps I was in a delirium in another body, another lifetime, or in my bed in Ohio.

I stopped and surveyed the forest below; the dark trees were highlighted by silver brush strokes of moonlight. No, this wasn't a dream; this was real sweat, and that was a real moon, and I was really tired. Soon, it would be dawn. The ridge was just above — another half hour, maybe. So I pushed on, racing the dawn to the top.

When I made it, breathing hard, I found a sheltered spot and slept until the sun peeked over the rocks and touched my face. I looked out over Molokai. Now what?

Soc's voice came to me then, in my memory. He had been speaking about the koan, an insolvable riddle designed to frustrate the conscious mind. The "solution" or answer was not the right words, but the insight behind them.

I wondered if Mama Chia's riddle was a koan, as well. A part of my mind began to contemplate this question, and would continue contemplating it many hours, whether I was awake or asleep.

Then I thought about shape-shifting. Mama Chia had called it a "deep form of empathy." When I was a child, I had played "what-if" games: What if I were a tiger — what would that be like? What if I were a gorilla? And in my own childlike way, I would mimic these beasts, not skillfully, but with real feeling. Maybe that would help me now.

As that idea came to me, I saw an albatross, flying quite low, soaring on a thermal, sitting almost stationary in the air above me. With a shock, I realized that for a single instant I had become the albatross, seeing through its eyes, looking down at me. With a loud caw, the bird flew, in a straight line, as if coasting down an endless slide, toward another town. And I knew the next place I would go — yes — the town of Kuanakakai. What a miraculous night!

Before I started my descent, I surveyed the entire island, bathed in moonlight. It's perfect that I came here, first, to get an overview, I thought. I was about to leave when I noticed a feather of the albatross at my feet. I picked it up, then felt an ancient urge rising inside me. I was beginning a quest — why not start with a ceremony?

I raised the feather over my head with my left arm, and pointed my right arm to the ground — connecting heaven and earth. I felt, and looked, like the magician card of a tarot deck I remembered. Then, I saluted the North, the South, the East, and the West and asked the island spirits for assistance.

My Basic Self gave me renewed strength as I headed down, as quickly as my legs could carry me. I stopped only once for a brief rest, in the late morning, picking some papayas on the way, tearing them open, eating them sloppily, with no regard for manners, and tossing the skins to enrich the soil. I walked with a vengeance, with a purpose, although I had no idea yet what it was. Ah, yes, I told myself. Going to town.

A helpful rainsquall washed the papaya juice from my face and hands and chest; then the sun dried me, and the wind blow-dried my hair and beard.

I hitched a ride partway in the back of a pickup truck with "Molokai Ranch" stenciled on the side, and I walked the rest of the way to Kaunakakai. I felt quite the rugged mountain man when I sauntered into town — straight into the arms, so to speak, of my recent acquaintance and old nemesis, Beer Belly, along with his companions.

By this time, I wasn't totally grounded, to say the least. Up most of the night, fueled by a few papayas, I felt past tired — approaching punch-drunk. As the glow of recognition slowly filled Beer Belly's round face and his fists started clenching, I heard myself say, in my best cowboy voice, "I hear you bushwhackers bin' lookin' fer me."

This stopped their advance for the moment. "Bushwakas," mused Beer Belly. "Dis guy called us 'bushwakas.'"

"I don' think dat's good," one of his larger friends volunteered.

"I don' pay you to think," their fearless leader announced.

"You don' pay me at all," Big Fella retorted in a stroke of genius. I noticed that the smallest of these young gentlemen outmatched me by six inches and maybe fifty pounds.

As their discussion continued, Beer Belly recalled his original intent and inspiration: to turn me into poi. Usually you mash up taro root into a white paste, but I would do fine, I believed he surmised, as he stepped forward to clean my chops.

Beer Belly swung and I managed to draw upon enough of my recent training to dodge the blow, rolling with that punch, and the next, and the next. He threw punches like a major-league pitcher — speedballs, curves, and baseline screamers. My Basic Self must have learned its lessons well. Force comes in, get out of the way, I thought, evading each punch.

I was no martial arts master after one lesson. But it had been a very good lesson. And if the truth be known, Beer Belly may have already had a few too many and was not really at his best.

I had to hand it to this kid; he was persistent. Turning red in the face, huffing and puffing, he tried to swat this hippie *haole* boy, probably from California. And he was failing. In front of his friends.

I continued slipping and bobbing and weaving, starting to feel like Bruce Lee. I even had time to send a silent thanks to Fuji.

Then I remembered something else Fuji had taught me: Sometimes, the best way to win a fight is to lose it.

Instantly, I turned in to this young fellow, I felt what he was feeling, and I grew sad. This was his domain I had invaded — and fighting was one of the few things he prided himself in, and he was falling apart in front of the only friends he had. As usual, I'd only been thinking about me. Fuji was right. An important part of self-defense is knowing when not to defend the self.

I let down my guard and rolled with the punch as Beer Belly, with one last heroic effort, let loose a right hook that glanced off my cheekbone. It was like getting hit with a flying ham. I heard a loud sound as my head snapped to the side; I saw stars and found myself lying on a pile of scattered trash.

Half sitting up, rubbing my head, I said, "That was one hell of a punch. You have brass knuckles, or what?"

He had saved face. I was the vanquished enemy. I saw his expression change as he held up his fist.

"Deez knuckles made of *iron,*" he said.

"Help me up, will you?" I said, reaching up. "Let me buy you guys a beer."

CHAPTER 21

Sunlight Under the Sea

In the sea caves, there's a thirst, there's a love,
there's an ecstasy, all hard like shells,
you can hold them in your palm.

— George Seferis, *Book of Exercises*

HE HESITATED, then reached down and pulled me up. "I can drink a lot of beer," he said with a smile that revealed two missing teeth. As we walked toward the store — the sign over the door said "Spirits" — I rubbed my bruised cheekbone, glad for the ten-spot Fuji had given me, since I had almost no other cash. I thought to myself, This is one hell of a way to make new friends.

But make new friends I did. Especially with Beer Belly, whose real name was Kimo. He seemed to take a liking to me, too. The other guys drifted off after my money ran out, but Kimo stayed around. He even offered to buy me one.

"Oh, thanks, Kimo, but I'm full up — hey," I said on impulse, "do you know where I can get hold of a sailboat?" I really don't know where that idea came from, but I was going, as they say, with the flow.

To my surprise, Kimo, who had been staring at the bar and sipping his beer, came alive. His cheeks got more colorful, and he turned to me, excited as a young schoolkid. "You wanna sail? I got a boat. I'm the best sailor in dis town."

To put it mildly, we were out of there. And half an hour later, we were cruising out to sea on a stiff breeze, bouncing over the slight chop. "I know dis good spot for fishin'. You like fishin'?" This question was, of course, purely rhetorical, as if he'd said, "You like breathin'?" — leaving little room for a negative response.

"I haven't been fishing in years," I said diplomatically. As it turned out, there was one rod, so Kimo fished, lost in his own world, and I, glad for the company, leaned over the side and gazed beneath the surface.

The chop had calmed to a glassy surface; the water was clear as crystal. I saw schools of fish swimming below, and wondered what it would be like...

WITHOUT ANY CONSCIOUS EFFORT on my part — maybe that was the key — I found my awareness flying with the fish. That's what it was — flying. To the fish, the sea is air. I felt an unaccustomed sense of aquatic mastery; with a flick of my tailfin, I was a rocket, a shooting star. The next moment, I was totally relaxed and gliding...

Relaxed, but always alert. Death came from any direction here, and suddenly. I saw a larger fish snap and a smaller one was gone. The sea was a living machine of movement and reproduction, eating and death, but in spite of it all, great beauty, and peace.

I SNAPPED BACK AS KIMO SAID, "You know, Dan, dis boat — and dis ocean — it feels like my life."

Sensing that he was sharing something personal, I listened intently.

"Seem like sometime it's peaceful — like now. Udder times dere's a storm — can't control da storm — but can trim da sail, tie things down, get tru dat storm and you're a lot stronger — you know?"

"Yeah, I know what you mean, Kimo. My life's a lot like that, too."

"Yeah?"

"Yeah. I guess we've all got our storms," I said.

He grinned at me. "You're all right, you know? I didn't think so, before. But I do, now."

I grinned back at him. "I think you're all right, too." I really meant it; Kimo seemed like a different person, now that I had looked beneath the surface.

Kimo was about to say something else, I could tell. He hesitated, maybe working up the nerve, then confided, "Someday, I'm gonna finish high school, an' get a good job. Learn to speak betta, like you." He waited. Somehow, my opinion meant something to him.

"Well," I said, "anyone who understands the sea as well as you do — I think he can do any damn thing he sets his mind to."

I saw a glow spread across his face. "You really think so?"

"I really think so."

Thoughtful, he didn't say anything for a while, so I just sat and gazed into the clear water below. Then, abruptly, he pulled in his fishing rod and set sail. "Dere's someplace I wanna show you." Tacking, we headed south, until we came to a reef, just visible beneath the water's surface.

Kimo trimmed the sail, kicked off his thongs, and dove into the water like a seal. His head quickly reappeared. Clearly in his element, he reached inside the boat, grabbed a diving mask, threw me a pair of goggles, and said, "Come on in!"

"You bet!" I said enthusiastically. Sweaty and dirty, I needed a swim. I slipped off my shirt, rid myself of my sneakers and socks, adjusted and slipped on the goggles, and followed him as he glided smoothly through the water, directly over the beautiful, razor-edged coral reef, about ten feet below the surface.

Kimo swam about twenty yards more, then stopped, treading water, and waited for me. Not being a very strong swimmer, I felt the exertion; by the time I reached him and started treading water like a landlubber, I was already tired. So I had my doubts when he said, "Follow me down."

"Wait a minute," I said, panting, wishing I'd spent more time doing laps at the college pool. "What's down there?"

So at home in the water himself, Kimo didn't really appreciate that I might not be entirely comfortable. But he saw my doubtful expression and, floating on his back, otterlike, he explained, "Dere's a cave. Nobody knows about it but me. I'm gonna show it to you."

"But, it's underwater. How're we going to breathe?"

"At first you gotta hold your breath. But once we get tru da tunnel, we come up in dis cave, an' dere's *air,"* he said, sharing his discovery with growing excitement.

Far less enthusiastic, I asked, "How long do we have to hold our br — ?" He suddenly turned bottom up and dove straight down beneath the shimmering surface. "Kimo!" I yelled after him. "How long is the tunnel?"

I had a few seconds to make my decision. Would I follow him, or just swim back to the boat? That was safer, and probably wiser. But that little voice I'd heard many times before, said, *Go for it!*

"Oh, shut up!" I heard myself say aloud, as I took some deep, rapid breaths, and dove, following Kimo.

The goggles fit okay, and I was actually more relaxed underwater than trying to hold myself above. And all the breathing exercises I'd done in the past, and the few I did daily, helped. I could take a deep breath and hold it longer than most people, but not necessarily while swimming fifteen feet down, then through a tunnel that went who knows how far.

My ears started hurting from the pressure. I held my nose and blew, then stroked madly to catch up with Kimo, focusing all the while on that cave, with air. I saw him go into a large hole in the side of the reef, and I followed him into the dim light.

To my dismay, the tunnel narrowed as we swam; I carefully avoided the sharp coral. A mental image of an eel made me look right and left into the many dark spaces that could hold a sea creature. My lungs told me it was time to breathe — now — but the tunnel continued as far as I could see. Then, it began to narrow even more. In a moment of panic, I realized I couldn't turn around. My lungs were pumping madly, but I clamped my lips together and fought on.

I saw Kimo's feet disappear, and just as my mouth was about to burst open to feel the choking water rush in, I angled upward, then gasped like a newborn infant as my head emerged into the air of an underwater cavern.

My mood much improved, I lay panting, half submerged, on a rock ledge.

"Some kinda place, huh?" he asked.

"Uh huh," I managed to say. Recovering, I looked up and around at purple, green, and blue coral, dramatically colored as if it had been decorated by a movie set designer. Then I noticed something odd: A single beam of sunlight shone through the roof of the cave. But the whole reef was underwater! How could there be an opening?

"You noticed da light, huh?" Kimo said. "Up dere, in da ceiling — see dat piece of glass? It covers an opening, so da water don't come in."

"How — ?"

"*Ama* — Japanese divers from a long time ago, I think. Maybe dey explore dis cave — put da glass dere," he pointed.

I nodded, still puzzled. "But how did the air get in here?

"Comes in a few times a year when da tide's low. Sometimes it leaks. I first foun' dis place when I saw some tiny bubbles coming up to da surface."

Feeling better, I sat up, and felt the excitement of being in this hidden alcove, safe from the world. We grinned at each other like two boys in their secret clubhouse. "Do you think anyone else has ever been here?" I asked.

Kimo shrugged. "Jus' dose *ama* divers an' me."

We were silent after that, gazing in awe, feeling the energy of this underwater cave where the sunlight streamed in.

Kimo lay back and stared at the ceiling. I explored, crawling carefully over the sharp coral. In this subsea tide pool, algae and seaweed grew thick, clinging to the coral, giving the cave an eerie greenish hue.

I was turning to crawl back, when my arm slipped. It plunged down into a crevice in the coral, right up to my shoulder. I was starting to extract my arm when my hand closed around something — maybe a chunk of rock. I pulled it out, opened my hand, and was amazed to see what appeared to be a small statue, so encrusted with tiny barnacles and algae it was hard to be sure. "Look at this!" I called to Kimo.

He came over and looked at it, as awestruck as I. "Looks like a statue or something," he said.

"Here," I said, handing it to him. I didn't want to give it away, but it seemed the right thing to do.

He looked at it, and clearly would have liked it, but he had his standards, too. "No. You found it. You keep it. To remember."

"Thanks for showing me this cave, Kimo."

"You keep it a secret, okay?"

"I'll never tell anyone where it is," I promised, tucking the statue into my pants.

The swim out was challenging, but not as difficult as the way in, because now I knew how far it was, and had time to rest and take many deep breaths to prepare.

By the time we got back to shore, it was getting dark. Kimo insisted that I could stay at his place. So I got to meet his three sisters and four brothers, two of whom I'd already met with him on the street. They all nodded, curious or oblivious, as they passed quickly through the room in which we sat and talked. He offered me a beer, which I accepted, and sipped slowly, and some pungent weed he called "Maui Mindblow," which I declined.

We talked late into the night, and I got to understand the soul of another human being very different from me, yet the same.

Before Kimo flopped onto his unmade sleeper bed and I stretched out on some blankets on the floor, he shared something else with me: He told me how he'd felt different from other people his whole life, "like I was from another place or something," he added. "And I got a feeling dere's something I'm supposed to do wit' my life, only I don't know what..." he trailed off.

"Maybe finish high school first," I said. "Or sail the seven seas."

"Yeah," he said, closing his eyes. "Sail the seven seas."

As I drifted off to sleep, I thought back on this incredible day: starting out on a mountaintop, ending with Kimo and the underwater cave. And finding that barnacle-encrusted statue, now safe in my pack. I'd have to examine it more closely the next chance I got.

IN THE MORNING, I said good-bye to Kimo and I set out alone, back into the rain forests of Molokai, toward Pelekunu Valley. I had the feeling that the "treasure" Mama Chia had spoken of might be absorbed in little bits and pieces, not all at once, but that they might add up to something. And if I just stayed alert and open, and traveled where my heart led, I would find the rest of the treasure, whatever it was.

As I walked along the back roads, getting short rides with a rancher or town person, and then entered the forest, I thought about Kimo, and the other people I'd met, from all walks of life. Remembering my vision in the fire, I wondered about their purpose, and how we all fit into the bigger picture. Someday I'd find the tools to help them understand, and to find that purpose. I knew this, if I knew anything.

WALKING AFTER DARK in a strange part of the rain forest, I felt disoriented, and suddenly weary. Not wanting to travel in circles, I decided to sleep where I was until the first light of dawn, then continue. I lay down and fell quickly asleep, with a vague feeling of ill ease, as if maybe I shouldn't be there, but it was only a very subtle feeling, and it was probably just my fatigue.

In the night, I had a strange and dark but compelling sexual dream. A succubus — a female seductress — both darkly dangerous and terribly erotic, came to love me...to death. She wore a filmy blue gown that revealed creamy skin.

I half woke up, and realized where I was, but an icy feeling of horror gripped me as I felt her presence and then saw a woman's shape, blue and gauze covered, floating, moving toward me through the trees. I quickly looked left and right and saw that I had stumbled into a place of unmarked burials, and restless souls.

The hairs stood up on the back of my neck as my Basic Self told me to get out of there. *Now.*

As the spirit's cold, shapely form floated closer, I could sense that fear and seduction were her only powers, but I had been prepared for this; I had returned from hell, and neither fear nor seduction had the same power over me. *"You'll not have me,"* I said with authority. "I'm not here for you."

I forced myself to wake up fully, and I walked slowly out of that place, not looking back, knowing all the time that she was following me, close behind.

At some point, I felt her give up and fall away, but I kept walking through the rest of the night, just the same. Something else was troubling me — a vague feeling again, like I was missing something important. But this time the feeling clarified, like a word on the tip of my tongue.

A phrase from Mama Chia's riddle came to mind: "As above, then so below." Now what could that mean?

I was "above" in the highlands. I was "below" in the town. I had been "beneath the sea." It was all the same. As above, so below. Different, yet the same. Because wherever I went, I was there! The treasure wasn't in any one of these places; it was in *all* of them. Mama Chia had already told me the answer; it was inside me — as close as my own heart.

This was more than an intellectual understanding. It hit me with an overwhelming force, an ecstatic realization. For a moment, I lost all awareness of my body. I collapsed on the wet leaves. I had found the treasure, the most important secret of all. Energy welled up inside me. I wanted to cry, to dance!

But in the next moment, ecstasy gave way to another feeling: a sudden sense of loss. And I knew, without knowing how, that Mama Chia was dying. "No!" I cried into the trees. "No. Not yet. Please, wait for me!"

I got to my feet and started to run.

CHAPTER 22

Living Until We Die

True teachers use themselves as bridges
over which they invite their students to cross;
then, having facilitated their crossing, joyfully collapse,
encouraging them to create bridges of their own.

— Nikos Kazantzakis

I DON'T KNOW HOW LONG I RAN, climbed, scrambled, and ran
again. Covered with mud, exhausted, cut and bruised, then
cleansed by a heavy rain, I finally stumbled and fell at the foot of
Mama Chia's stairs about two hours after sunrise.

Fuji, Mitsu, Joseph, and Sarah came out, and Joseph helped
me inside. Mama Chia was lying peacefully on the futon bed,
surrounded by flowers.

My friends, supporting me at first, stepped back as I went to
her and knelt by the bed, my head bowed and tears streaming
down my cheeks. I rested my forehead on her arm, so cool, so cool.

I couldn't speak at first; stroking her face, I said farewell, and
offered a silent prayer. Mitsu sat nearby, stroking Sachi, comforting her. Socrates, in the blissful ignorance of childhood, slept next
to his sister.

Joseph looked like a sad Don Quixote, his eyes dark, one hand on Sarah's shoulder as she rocked in grief.

A stillness pervaded the valley, a sadness, unbroken by the cries of Redbird, the *'apapane*. Here had passed a very special woman. Even the birds were in mourning.

Just then, the *'apapane* landed on the windowsill, tilted his head to one side, and looked at Mama Chia. Birds have a cry of sadness, and we heard it that morning — an unaccustomed sound — as Redbird flew to her side, made the call again, and flew away, like her soul.

I walked into the moist warm air toward the east, the rising sun just now lighting the sky, silhouetting the hills. Joseph walked with me. "She must have died quietly, in the night," he told me. "Fuji found her only an hour ago. Dan, we heard you were away; how did you know?"

I gazed up at him, and my eyes told him what he needed to know.

Nodding in understanding, Joseph told me, "Some time ago, she left me instructions," he said, "about where to take Tia's baby, and other business matters. She asked to be cremated, in the burial ground of the kahunas. I'll be making the arrangements."

"I want to help with anything I can — with everything," I told him.

"Yes, of course — if you wish. Oh, and there was this," he revealed, holding up a piece of paper. "I think she wrote you this last night."

We looked at the note; in Mama Chia's scrawled handwriting were six words: "Among friends, there are no good-byes."

I went back inside, sat near her, and just looked at her. When I was young, death was a stranger to me — a phone call, a letter, a piece of information, a solemn announcement about people I rarely saw. Death was a visitor to other homes, other places. People just faded into memory.

But this was real, and it hurt like a razor cut. Sitting there, with the body of Mama Chia, Death whispered into my ears with cold breath, bringing intimations of my own mortality.

I stroked her cheek, feeling an ache in my heart that no metaphysical philosophy could remedy. I missed her already; I felt the void she left, as if a piece of my life had been taken away. And I reflected that, ultimately, we have no control in this life — no ability to stop the waves that come crashing down. We can only learn to surf those waves, embracing whatever comes and using it to grow. Accepting ourselves, our strengths and weaknesses, our foolishness and our love. Accepting everything. Doing what we can, and flowing with the rest.

It may seem strange to some people that I would be so attached to a woman I'd only met a short time before, but my admiration for Mama Chia — for her goodness and courage and wisdom — made up for the brief time of our acquaintance, and made her passing all the more painful. Perhaps I'd known her for lifetimes. She was one of my most beloved teachers who had somehow been waiting for me since my birth.

JOSEPH CONTACTED MAMA CHIA'S SISTER, who informed her other relatives. We let the body rest for two days, as Mama Chia had requested. Then, on the third morning, we prepared for the trek up Pelekunu Valley to the sacred kukui grove and the burial site beyond. The old pickup truck became her hearse, decorated with leis and garlands of flowers. We drove carefully over the makeshift roads as far east as the roads would carry us — Fuji and I, followed by Joseph, Sarah, Mitsu, with her little boy, and Joseph's family, as well as Victor, her nieces, other relatives, and a long procession of the many local people Mama Chia had known and helped over the years.

When the road ended, we carried her on the pallet, constructed by her friends from the leper colony, on slippery, winding paths, past waterfalls through the kukui forest she had loved so well, into the burial site of the kahunas. The lepers were still restricted to their compound, and so couldn't accompany us, but they sent many flowers.

We entered the burial ground in the late afternoon. I felt the ancient kahuna spirit, Lanikaula, welcome Mama Chia, welcome us all, as I knew he would. Now they would both stand eternal watch over the island they loved.

By dusk, we had built her funeral pyre as she had instructed, setting her on a bed of leaves and flower petals, atop many logs, crisscrossed beneath her, gathered from a dry part of the island.

As the pyre was prepared, some of those closest to her said a few words in memorial, or recited quotations that reminded them of Mama Chia.

Fuji was overcome, and couldn't speak; his wife, Mitsu, said, "This is what Mama Chia taught me: We cannot always do great things in life, but we can do small things with great love."

Joseph, quoting Buddha, said, "Gifts are great; meditations and religious exercises pacify the mind; comprehension of the great truth leads to nirvana; but greater — " Here, he began to cry. "But greater than all is loving kindness."

Never taking her sad eyes off the pyre, Sachi said, simply, "I love you, Mama Chia."

Another woman, a stranger to me, said, "Mama Chia taught me that kind words can be short and easy to speak, but their echoes are endless." Then she sank to her knees and bowed her head in prayer.

When my turn came, my mind went completely blank. I had prepared something to say, but it was gone. I stared another long moment, in silence, at the pyre, as images flashed through my mind — meeting Ruth Johnson on the street, then at the party, then as she nursed me back to health — and then a long-forgotten quotation from Matthew came to me: "I was hungry and you fed me; I was thirsty and you gave me water; I was a stranger and you welcomed me; naked and you clothed me; ill and you comforted me." I spoke these words not just for me, but for all the people gathered there.

Fuji came up to me, and to my surprise, handed me the torch. "She asked in her instructions that you light the pyre, Dan, if you were still here on Molokai. She said you'd know how to give her a good send-off." He smiled sadly.

I lifted the torch. And I understood that everything she had shown me came to this: Live until you die.

"Good-bye, Mama Chia," I said aloud. I touched the torch to the dry grass and sticks, and the flames began to crackle and dance. And the body of Mama Chia, covered with a thousand petals of red and white and pink and purple, was embraced by the flames, and engulfed.

As the smoke rose to the sky, I stepped back from the blazing heat. Then, in the dying light of day, as this small group of people gazed into the flames, I recalled how Mama Chia enjoyed quoting sources of wisdom, and from out of nowhere, the words of George Bernard Shaw came to me — words she herself might have said — and I found myself calling them out loudly above the crackle of the roaring fire for all to hear: "I want to be thoroughly used up when I die, for the harder I work, the more I live. I rejoice in life for its own sake. Life is no 'brief candle' to me; it is a sort of splendid torch which I have got hold of for the moment, and I want to make it burn as brightly as possible — " My voice quivered then, and I could speak no more.

Others spoke, as Spirit moved them, but I heard none of it. I cried, and I laughed, as Mama Chia would have laughed; then I fell to my knees and bowed my head. My heart was open, my mind silent.

I LOOKED UP SUDDENLY because I heard Mama Chia's voice, as loud and clear as if she were standing in front of me. All the others still had their heads bowed, or were staring at the fire, and I realized that the words resounded only in the quiet halls of my mind. In her soft, sometimes lilting voice, Mama Chia spoke to me, and said:

> Do not stand at my grave and weep.
> I am not there; I do not sleep.
> I am a thousand winds that blow.
> I am the diamond glints on snow.
> I am the sunlight on ripened grain.
> I am the gentle autumn rain.
> Do not stand at my grave and cry.
> I am not there. I did not die.

When I heard these words, my heart broke open and my awareness leaped to a place I had never been before. I felt the nature of mortality and death within the great circle of life. Overwhelmed, I swooned with a searing compassion for all living things. I fell at once into the depths of despair and soared to the heights of bliss — these two feelings alternated within me at the speed of light.

Then, I was no longer on Molokai, but standing in the tiny room I had seen in my vision under the waterfall. Acrid, pungent smells of sewage and decay filled the air, partly masked by burning incense. I saw a nun caring for a bedridden leper. In the blink of an eye, I became the nun, wearing heavy robes in the sweltering heat. I reached out to smooth an ointment on this poor man's face, my heart completely opened to the love, to the pain, to everything. And in the leper's disfigured face, I saw the faces of all those I had ever loved.

The next moment I stood on the rue de Pigalle, watching a gendarme help a sick, drunken man into a police ambulance. Then I became that police officer, I smelled the drunkard's putrid breath. A light flashed, and I saw the drunkard as a child, huddled in a corner, quaking as his own father, in a drunken rage, lashed out at him. I felt his pain, his fear — all of it. Looking through the gendarme's eyes, I carried the drunkard gently to the waiting van.

The next moment, I found myself gazing, as if through a mirror, at a teenage boy in his bedroom in a wealthy suburb of Los Angeles. He was sniffing powder up his nose. I knew his guilt, and regret, and self-hatred. Then I felt only compassion.

Next, I was in Africa, gazing at an old man, moving painfully, trying to give a dying baby water. I cried out, and my voice echoed in this timeless place where I stood. I cried for that baby, for the old African, for the teenage boy, for the drunken man, for the nun, for the leper. That baby was my child, and these were my people.

I wanted so much to help, to make things better for every suffering soul, but I knew that from where I stood I could only love, understand, trust in the wisdom of the universe, do what I could, then let go.

As I saw all this, I felt an explosive surge of energy, and I was catapulted up, through my heart, in a state of perfect empathy with existence itself.

My body had become transparent, radiating shifting colors of the spectrum. Below, I felt red, rising through orange, and yellow, and green, changing into gold. Then, surrounded by a radiant blue, my inner eyes were drawn up to the center of my forehead, rising into indigo, then violet...

Beyond the confines of personal identity, no longer concerned with a physical body, I floated in the place where spirit meets flesh, from a vantage point high above the planet we call earth. Then the earth receded in the vastness, then the solar system became a disappearing speck, and the galaxy, too, until I was beyond the illusions of space and matter and time, seeing It All: paradox, humor, and change.

What followed goes far beyond words. I can write that "I was One with the Light," but such words fall like dust on the page, because there was no "I" to be "One" with anything, and no one left to experience It. Trying to describe this experience has challenged and frustrated the mystic poets for centuries. How do you draw the likeness of a van Gogh painting with a stick in the mud?

The universe had burned me to cinders, consuming me. Not a trace remained. Only Bliss. Reality. Mystery.

Now I understood the Taoist saying "He who says does not know; he who knows does not say" — not because the wise don't speak, but because It cannot be spoken. Words fall as short of It as a rock thrown at the stars. And if these words sound nonsensical, so be it. But one day, and that day may not be far away, you, too, will know.

I REENTERED TIME AND SPACE — whirling, disoriented — as if I'd fallen out of an airplane in the night sky, still kneeling before Mama Chia's funeral pyre, set against the clouds that floated past the moon. The ground glistened from a fresh rain; I was soaking.

The rain had doused the last embers of the pyre that had consumed her. An hour had passed in a few moments.

The others had gone; only Joseph remained with me. He knelt down next to me and asked, "How are you doing, Dan?"

I couldn't speak, but I nodded. He gently squeezed the back of my neck; I could feel the love and understanding through his fingers. He knew I would be staying a while, so, with a last look at the charred pyre, he left.

I took a deep breath, smelling the wet forest, mixed with the lingering odor of smoke. None of it seemed completely real anymore, as if I were merely playing my role in an eternal drama, and this dimension was but one small practice hall in the infinite theater of God.

Slowly at first, questions trickled back into my mind, then came in a rush, as I fell from grace, back into the mind, into the body, into the world. What had it all meant?

Maybe this had been "the place beyond space and time" Mama Chia had told me about. At the time, her words had sounded abstract, empty, because they had been beyond my experience. Now they were a living reality. She had told me, "In that place, you can meet with anyone you wish." I wanted so much to go to that place again, just to see her one more time.

I stood, shaky and stiff, staring into space until darkness covered the forest.

Then I turned and started to follow the path taken by the others, back through the rain forest. High above, I could just make out the flow of the torch-lit procession.

But something wouldn't let me leave. The feeling was clear, so I sat down, and waited. I sat through the night, occasionally nodding out, then stirring again. Sometimes my eyes closed, as if in meditation; other times they just opened and stared.

WHEN THE FIRST RAYS OF SUNLIGHT cut through the forest and shone upon the remains of the pyre, Mama Chia appeared, tangible but translucent, standing in front of me. I don't know if any of the others would have seen her, or whether her image only appeared in my mind.

But there she stood. She raised her arm and pointed to the hillside on my right, gesturing toward a thick glade of trees.

"You want me to go up there?" I asked her aloud. She only smiled, serenely. I closed my eyes for a moment against the bright sun. When I opened them, she was gone.

From my altered — or perhaps refined — perception of reality, all this seemed entirely normal to me. I got up slowly, and went where she directed.

Still disoriented from the recent events and revelations, I wound my way through the thick bushes — caught once or twice on sticky vines — before the foliage thinned out and a narrow path appeared before me.

Lessons of Solitude

We must pass through solitude and difficulty, isolation and
silence, to find that enchanted place where we can dance our
clumsy dance and sing our sorrowful song. But in that dance,
and in that song, the most ancient rites of our conscience fulfill
themselves in the awareness of being human.

— Pablo Neruda, *Toward the Splendid City*

THE PATH LED TO A TINY HUT, about eight feet on each side. I
entered and surveyed the darkened interior. Only a few rays of sunshine penetrated the thatched roof and log walls. As my eyes
adjusted to the dim light, I saw, coming down through the ceiling,
a long, hollow piece of bamboo that carried rainwater, gathered on
the roof, into a large wooden tub sitting in one corner. In the opposite corner of this spartan room, I could make out a hole in the
ground that served as a toilet and a nearby bucket for flushing. The
earthen floor had a bed of thick leaves to one side for sleeping.

From the design of the hut, I assumed that it served as a place
of isolation and retreat. I decided to stay here until I received a
clear sign about what to do next.

I shut the thatched door behind me. Weary, I lay down and
closed my eyes.

Almost immediately, I sensed a nearby presence, and sat up. Mama Chia sat in front of me, her legs crossed, as if in meditation — but her eyes were open, and bright. I sensed that she wanted to communicate something, so I waited in silence, not wanting to disturb this tenuous apparition.

She gestured with a sweep of her arm, and I heard her say as her image began to flicker and fade, "Everything is a dream within a dream."

"I don't understand, Mama Chia. What does it mean?"

"We make our own meaning," she said as her image dissolved.

"Wait! Don't go!" I cried out. I wanted to touch her face, to embrace her; but I knew that this was neither appropriate nor possible.

In the darkness, I heard her final words, echoing from far away. "It's all right, Dan. Everything will be all right...." Then silence.

SHE WAS GONE — I could feel it in my bones. What would I do now? As soon as I asked the question, the answer appeared: There was nothing to do, except stay put and wait for clarity.

Surveying the narrow confines of my quarters, I took stock of my situation: I had no food, but I had dealt with that before. My Basic Self was no longer afraid of not eating, and the wooden tub contained plenty of water.

After a few lumbering stretches, I sat and closed my eyes. Soon, bits and pieces of memories, sights, and sounds replayed themselves in my mind, as I relived my entire adventure here in a random montage of fleeting images and emotions.

I recalled that Mama Chia had once told me, "Outer travel at best only reflects the inner journey, and at worst substitutes for it. The world you perceive only provides symbols for what you seek.

The sacred journey is inside you; before you can find what you're looking for in the world, you have to find it within. Otherwise, a master may greet you, but you'll walk right past without hearing.

"When you learn inner travel through the psychic spaces of the world, your consciousness will never again be limited by space, or time, or the confines of the physical body."

Although I had heard this before, only now did I understand it. Before I could continue my journey in the world, I had to journey within my psyche. Would I be able to accomplish this? Could my awareness go so deep within that it contacted the gateway beyond my physical senses?

I considered this intensely, that night and the following day. I had found Mama Chia in the forest. I knew that I had hidden capacities, as we all do. But where were they? What did they look like, and feel like?

Socrates had once hinted that there was "more to imagination than meets the eye." He said it was the "bridge to clairvoyant sight — a first step. As it expands," he added, "it becomes something else. Saplings grow into trees, but imagination is like the caterpillar — once set free of the cocoon, it flies."

I would begin there. I closed my eyes and let images float by: kukui trees and Kimo's underwater cave, the palm outside Mama Chia's house, and the thick, twisting trunk of the banyan. Then my daughter, Holly, appeared sitting in her room on the floor, playing quietly. I felt a bittersweet sadness at the karmas of this life, and I sent a message of love from my heart to hers, hoping that, in some way, she would receive it. I sent Linda my blessings, as well, and let go.

I SPENT THE ENTIRE NIGHT in vivid dreams — not surprising, considering recent events. I visited other places, worlds, and dimensions of color, clarity, and feeling that filled me with awe. But, of course — or so I thought — it was just a dream....

As one day followed the next, day and night ceased to have much distinction for me; the dim light of day only gave way to the darkness of night.

THE MORNING OF THE FIFTH DAY, as well as I could track time, brought a deep sense of lightness and peace. My hunger pangs had vanished. As I did a few yoga postures, the walls of the hut caught my eye as specks of sunlight penetrated the darkness like stars in a night sky. I used the specks of light on the wall as a meditation. As I breathed slowly, deeply, the stars began to fade, until I saw only my mind, projected against the darkness like a magic lantern show, a carousel of imagery and sound that played on and on. I spent the entire day gazing at the wall. Boredom ceased to exist as my awareness tuned in to finer, subtler energies. When you don't have TV, I reflected at one point, you find other things to do.

The days passed one like the next, yet never the same. I stretched, breathed, and watched the show. Rays of sunlight, then moonlight, swept slowly across the dirt floor like a pendulum of light. Time passed softly, with infinite slowness as I adjusted to the subtle rhythms and floated on an ocean of silence, disturbed only occasionally by the flotsam and jetsam of my mind.

At one point, something shifted; it was as if, in the face of my persistent awareness, a barrier fell away and a door opened. I understood how the Basic Self and Conscious Self, working together, provided the keys to motivation, discipline, healing, visualization, intuition, learning, courage, and power. In a few moments, I felt as if I'd digested an encyclopedia of metaphysics.

However, like the sorcerer's apprentice, I didn't know how to turn it off. Images flooded my mind until it went into overload.

My lungs began pumping like bellows, deeper, faster — the energy building until I thought I would burst.

My face started to tighten; I felt my lips curl back and, to my surprise, I growled like a wolf. Then my hands spontaneously moved into mudras, or postures, like those I had seen in India.

In the next moment, my mind stopped, and I found myself in the forest, face to face with the three selves: the childlike Basic Self, the robotlike Conscious Self, and the Higher Self, a being of radiant colors — swirling pink, indigo, deep violet hues. This being of light reached out with open arms to the other two.

Then the three selves merged.

I saw before me my own body — naked, except for a pair of shorts, illuminated by the pale moon, standing with arms spread wide. A reddish glow shone from the belly region, the head was a ball of light, and above the head iridescent colors swirled — reminding me of my vision on the beach so many weeks before.

This time, I entered the physical body that stood before me. I entered it fully, feeling the unity of its form. I felt the power of my navel, the purity of awareness illuminating the mind, and the inspiring call to ascend up into Spirit.

My long preparation had brought completion; the three selves had become one. There were no inner battles, no resistance within or without, so that my attention rested naturally and spontaneously in the heart. Whatever thoughts or images arose were dissolved there, in feeling and surrender. I became a point of awareness within the domain of the heart, rising up toward the crown of my head, to a point above and behind the brows.

I felt the healing, loving light of the Higher Self surround me, embrace me, pervading every cell and tissue down to the atomic structure. I heard its call, and felt a bridge of light stretching from that point of awareness that I am to the Higher Self, standing above and behind me. I felt its strength, its wisdom, its tenderness, its courage, its compassion, its mercy. I became aware of its connection to past and future, in the eternal present.

It called again, and I felt myself as that point of light, moving up the bridge, into the consciousness of my Higher Self. I moved within that form of light, watching over my physical form, below. My awareness and that of my Higher Self began to interpenetrate one another. I took in all of its qualities of serenity, strength, wisdom, and compassion.

I now knew what it knew, felt what it felt, as ecstatic waves of unbounded love flooded through me. I saw how angelic energies had crafted the body, and I understood the full opportunity that physical embodiment represents.

Just then, I became aware of other beings of light around my physical form. Waves of happiness washed through me as I realized I had known these beings since childhood, but had somehow ignored their presence. Some were fellow students, others were familiar images from forgotten dreams — angelic energies, healers, guides, and teachers — my spiritual family. I felt their love, and knew I would never again feel alone.

An angel of destiny stepped forward then, and raised its hands to offer symbols to guide me. I couldn't see its gifts until the hands of light came forward, into my vision, and opened. First I saw a bolt of lightning, then a heart. Then a golden eagle appeared, holding a laurel wreath in its talons. I recognized these as symbols of courage and love, the signs of the peaceful warrior.

Then, as its final gift, the angel revealed the shining image of a samurai warrior, his sword at his side — not standing, but kneeling in a meditative posture. Though I couldn't see his eyes, I felt they were open, and shining. Then the image faded. I thanked the angel of destiny for these gifts, and it, too, stepped back and dissolved.

From this place within the Higher Self consciousness, I knew that angels of wisdom, healing, and clarity are always available. I could look to the future, or past, and send love to anyone in the universe. And from this place, I could extend my vision effortlessly, beyond the physical body, and soar like an eagle.

With this revelation, I felt a pull back to my physical form; I felt my awareness ride down the bridge of light into the center of my forehead, and once again I became aware of the sounds of my nervous system, and of the beating of my heart.

Refreshed and at peace, I opened my physical eyes, feeling a rising wave of energy and bliss. In this state of deep reverie, I scratched a message on the floor:

There is no way to peace;
Peace is the Way.
There is no way to happiness;
Happiness is the Way.
There is no way to love;
Love is the Way.

IN THE DAYS THAT FOLLOWED, even in relatively normal consciousness, I started seeing clear images of places outside the hut, and in the world. My "imagination" could now take me further than I'd ever dreamed — to any world, any reality; the physical realm was only home base, the grounding place.

The universe had become my playground — filled with an infinite number of dimensions, times, spaces. I could be a knight in medieval Europe or a space adventurer in the fifty-eighth dimension; I could visit other worlds, or spend time within the molecules of a copper penny, because the awareness that we are can never be limited by time or space.

After this, I traveled every day — flying through the forest, or around the world. I visited my little daughter every day and saw her playing with new toys, or reading, or sleeping. No longer limited to the physical body, I now perceived it as only one of my domains. I could never again feel imprisoned by any walls, or by flesh and bones.

And I remembered what Mama Chia had told me: "You can speak of 'my body,' because you are not the body. You can also refer to 'my mind,' 'my selves,' 'my soul,' because you are not these things. You manifest as pure Awareness that shines through the human body, yet itself remains untouched and eternal.

"Awareness diffracts through the prism of the soul to become three forms of light — the three selves — each with a different kind of awareness uniquely suited to its purpose, function, and responsibilities.

"The Basic Self cares for and protects the physical body in cooperation with the other selves, providing support and balance. A foundation and vehicle for the soul's journey in the world, it connects the Conscious and Higher Selves to the earth like the roots of a tree.

"The Conscious Self guides, informs, interprets for, and sometimes reassures the Basic Self, as a parent would a child, educating it to best serve this embodiment. But this parent must cultivate loving ears to hear that child, respecting that child's individual spirit and growing awareness. Parenthood is a sacred training ground.

"The Higher Self radiates love, reminding, inspiring, and rekindling the spark of light within the Conscious Self, drawing it up into Spirit. It accepts the process of the Conscious Self, and waits, eternally patient and understanding.

"Each of the three selves is here to assist the others, integrating, forming a whole, greater than the sum of its parts."

THEN A MYSTICAL VISION played itself out in my mind, shedding light on her words: I saw a monk hiking through the foothills of a mountain range in late autumn. Multicolored leaves — red, orange, yellow, green — showered down from the branches, waving in the chill wind. Shivering, the monk found a cave and went inside, seeking shelter from the elements.

Inside the cave, the monk found a large bear. They looked each other over; for a few tense moments, the monk didn't know whether he would leave the cave alive. As the bear slowly approached him, the monk spoke. "Let us help each other, Brother Bear. If you let me live in this cave with you, and if you gather wood for the fire, I will bake bread for you every day." The bear agreed, and they became friends — the man always warm, the bear always fed.

The bear represented the Basic Self, and the monk, the Conscious Self. The fire, the bread, and the sheltering cave itself were all blessings of the Higher Self. Each aspect served the others.

AFTER MANY DAYS OF INNER TRAVEL, returning from far journeys, I came back to earth and into my human form. Then I remembered the final gift given to me by the angel of destiny. Before going to sleep, I asked my Basic Self to reveal to me what this gift might mean, and to show me in a way I might understand.

In the morning, I had my answer: I was told to examine the object I'd found in the underwater cave. All those loose ends came together, and I knew it was time to leave the hut.

I stepped outside and squinted as a flood of sunlight stung my eyes and poured through me. I smelled the forest after a fresh rain. I had been in solitude for twenty-one days.

Weak from lack of food, I walked slowly through the hills, feeling as if I weren't quite made of flesh and bones — like a newborn, fresh out of my thatched womb. With a deep breath, I surveyed the sights and sounds of a new world.

I knew that the peace and bliss I now experienced would pass. Once I returned to the everyday world, thoughts would return, but that was all right. I accepted my human condition. I would, like Mama Chia, live until I died. But for now, I bathed happily in the ecstasy of conscious rebirth.

I passed a papaya tree just as one of the fruits fell. I caught it, smiled, and thanked Spirit for all of its blessings, large and small. Chewing slowly, I inhaled the sweet aroma.

Then I noticed a tiny sprout nearby, rising through the red earth, pushing upward, toward the sun. Within the seed of this tiny sprout lay the mature tree and all the laws of nature. As that seed evolved, so would we all: Basic Selves evolving into Conscious Selves, expanding and refining their awareness; Conscious Selves rising through the heart to become Higher Selves by surrendering to the laws of Spirit; and Higher Selves evolving back into the very Light of Spirit.

And each lifts and guides that which is below; each supports that which is above.

If a tiny sprout could reveal this to me, would the sky some-day reveal its own secrets? And what could the stones tell me, or the trees whisper? Would I learn the way of the flowing stream, the ancient wisdom of the mountains? That was still to be discovered.

What did it all add up to? I remembered a story about Aldous Huxley. In his later years, a friend once asked him, "Professor Huxley, after all your spiritual studies and practice, what have you learned?"

His eyes still shining, he answered, "I can summarize all I've learned in six words: Try to be...a little kinder."

Little things make a big difference, I thought. And I breathed a sigh of compassion for those people, stuck in the details of life, who had, like me, lost sight of the bigger picture, the liberating truth at the core of our lives.

Then I remembered Mama Chia's final words: "It's all right, Dan. Everything will be all right."

My heart opened, and tears of happiness flowed, but also tears of sorrow for those who still feel alone, cut off, in their own huts of solitude. Then, in a rising wave, I laughed with joy, because I knew with absolute certainty that they, too, would be able to feel the love and support of Spirit — if only they would open the eyes of their heart.

There Are No Good-byes

There are no maps; no more creeds or philosophies.
From here on in, the directions come straight from the Universe.

— Akshara Noor

As soon as I returned to my cabin, I reached into my pack and took out the encrusted object from Kimo's cave. I spent several hours cleaning it, carefully scraping with my Swiss Army knife. After numerous washings and scrubbings, I began to make out, with growing understanding and awe, the shape of a samurai warrior, kneeling in meditation — revealing the next step on my journey — to Japan, or somewhere in Asia, where I would find the master of the hidden school.

That night, I dreamed of an elderly man, an Asian, his face sad and wise. Something weighed heavily on his heart. Behind him, acrobats somersaulted through the air. And I knew I would find him — not only to receive, but to serve.

I SAID QUIET FAREWELLS, without ceremony, to each of the friends who had become so dear to me — to Joseph and Sarah, to Sachi and little Socrates, to Fuji and Mitsu with their baby, and to Manoa, Tia, and the others I'd come to know and care about deeply.

Joseph had told me the location of a small boat Mama Chia had left for me, anchored in a shallow cove hidden by trees at Kalaupapa, the leper colony. This time, I brought sufficient provisions to take me home. On a warm morning in November, with the sun rising out of the sea, I tossed my pack under the seat, slid the boat down the sand into the shallow surf, and climbed in. A breeze caught the sail.

Out past the surf, on the gentle rise and fall of the sea, I looked back to see rain streaking the cliffs with myriad cascades, some exploding into wind-whipped mist and rainbows before they reached the sea.

A larger rainbow, glorious in its colors, formed and stretched the length of the island as it arched across the sky. Then, gazing once more toward shore, just for a moment, I saw the limping figure of a large, rounded woman emerging from the curtain of trees through the mist. Her hand raised in farewell, then she was gone.

I TURNED FORWARD, into the wind, tacking across the channel toward Oahu.

On that little island of Molokai, guided by an unexpected teacher, I had seen the invisible world, the larger view of life, with eyes that see no duality — no "me" and "others," no separate self, no light or shadow, nothing within or without not made of Spirit — and that vision would illuminate all the days of my life.

I knew the visions and experiences would fade, and the restless feeling would continue, because my journey wasn't over — not yet. I would return home to see my daughter, clear up unfinished business, and put my affairs in order, just in case. Then I would find the school in Japan, and discover another part of Socrates' and Mama Chia's past — and my own future. Throwing my life to the winds, I would follow, once again, where Spirit leads.

THE ISLAND BEGAN TO FADE, then disappear under the cover of clouds. A gust of wind filled the sail, and a sweet fragrance perfumed the air. I looked up, gazing with wonder, as flower petals of every color rained down from the sky. Awestruck, I shut my eyes. When I opened them again, the petals had vanished. Had this shower really happened? Did it matter?

Smiling, I gazed out to sea. About a hundred yards away, a great humpback whale, rarely seen this time of year, breached the surface and slapped the water with its magnificent tail, sending a wave to greet me, pushing me onward, sending me surfing, like the ancient Hawaiian kings, toward home. And I knew that, like this small boat, Spirit would carry me, as it carries us all, inexorably, toward the Light.

A Special Afterword
for the Revised Edition

I want you to feel what I felt.
I want you to know why story-truth
is truer sometimes than happening-truth.

— Tim O'Brien, *The Things They Carried*

ONE OF THE GREAT BLESSINGS of fiction is that it enables us, both reader and writer, to live more than one lifetime — to inhabit different bodies and lives — to gain experience and perspectives we might never see through our own eyes.

Now that you've read this story, it has become part of your story, and Mama Chia is now a part of you, too. And, if you've read *Way of the Peaceful Warrior,* Socrates is also your teacher and a part of your experience. I am glad to have the opportunity to share my teachers with you in this way, because we are ultimately in this together.

Every book has a deeper tale to tell about its conception and birth. And now I can relate some of that story. In the process, you may find some truths about my life that shed light on your own.

While much of this work is fiction, I did receive a grant from Oberlin College to travel around the world. I did travel to Hawaii and experienced, in one form or another, elements similar to those described in this book. But in contrast to what I implied in earlier editions of this book, I never left my family for years in order to "find myself." In fact, I traveled only through the summer. But those three months changed the course of my life.

On the first leg of my journey, I participated in a forty-day intensive training created by a Bolivian master, exploring a unique array of practices, including meditation techniques, relaxation, breath work, concentration, and tools of self-observation. This experience contributed to an expanded awareness, a more relaxed and energized body, and a greater openness to the Divine Spirit that pervades self and world.

All of that occurred more than thirty years ago. Things change; everything has its time. I've since set aside esoteric methodologies to simply live in direct relationship with life as it unfolds, moment to moment. Daily life has become my spiritual practice, and this moment has become my life.

Each of us, particularly those of us involved in the arena of personal and spiritual growth, are shaped by our own specific lineage of mentors and life experience. In my case, each new source opened a floodgate of information, insight, and practice that generated, in turn, a new phase of my teaching work. After learning the way of the Hawaiian kahunas, I intended to write a sixty-page booklet entitled "Awakening the Three Selves." But then I thought: Why not use Molokai as the setting of a story? Thus, *Sacred Journey* was born, and a new teacher, Mama Chia, came into being.

While the character of Socrates is based upon a wise old mechanic I met in a service station decades ago, Mama Chia is a composite character, comprised of impressions and memories of wise, women I've known. I wrote *Sacred Journey* to convey a clear understanding of the three selves, and to describe, in a fresh way, that ascending scale of human awareness and evolution known in Chinese and Hindu traditions as the chakras.

Since 1990, after the first edition of *Sacred Journey* was published, whenever I was exposed to unique models, methods, or other illumined perspectives, I would, as Socrates had advised, integrate the material into my own life until I had sufficient clarity to write about it. My books *No Ordinary Moments, The Life You Were Born to Live, The Laws of Spirit,* and those that followed reflect these successive waves of insight and information.

But after all the methods, models, theories, and esoteric "secrets" are revealed, one eternal law of reality remains: The quality of our lives is shaped by what we do, moment to moment — by each choice we make and each action we take. Will we choose the main highways or the back roads of life? Will we travel the mountain paths or seek the forest wilderness? Will we contract or expand, struggle with or embrace life unfolding? Each of us must answer such questions for ourselves and make our own choices on this sacred journey, as the winding path appears beneath our feet.

My next book in the *Peaceful Warrior* saga will be a major novel about the life of Socrates — how the peaceful warrior found his way. And as the years unfold, I intend to write more stories that reflect the triumphs and heartbreaks that remind us of our common humanity, our courage, our spirit.

Dan Millman
Spring 2004

Acknowledgments

I WROTE THIS STORY IN SOLITUDE, yet any book is a collaborative venture, completed with the support of editor, designer, typesetter, research assistants, initial manuscript readers who provided feedback, and former teachers on whose shoulders I stand.

My deep appreciation to the following people who contributed, directly or indirectly, to this manuscript: Michael Bookbinder, editor Nancy Grimley Carleton, research assistant Sandra Knell, Hawaiian historian Richard Marks. Special thanks to my friends and publishers Hal and Linda Kramer for their encouragement and enthusiasm, and for this new edition, my appreciation also to Munro Magruder, Jason Gardner, Mary Ann Casler, Kristen Cashman, Michael Ashby, Monique Muhlenkamp, Cathey Flickinger, Tona Pearce Myers, and the team at New World Library.

As always, love and gratitude to my wife, Joy, who for three decades has illuminated my life.

About the Author

DAN MILLMAN'S BOOKS have inspired millions of readers in twenty-nine languages worldwide.

A graduate of the University of California at Berkeley, he is a former world trampoline champion, Stanford gymnastics coach, and Oberlin College professor. In 1994, he was inducted into the USA Gymnastics Hall of Fame.

Years ago, Dan traveled around the world, practicing various forms of yoga, martial arts, and other methods of personal and spiritual growth. He studied with an unusual array of teachers. Over time, he began to write and speak about ways to cultivate a peaceful heart with a warrior's spirit, using the challenges of daily life as a means of personal evolution and global transformation.

For two decades he has spoken to groups small and large, across America and around the world. His talks and trainings continue to influence leaders in business, health, psychology, education, politics, sports, and the arts. His practical approach to living has helped countless men and women to clarify and energize their personal and professional lives.

Dan continues to reach across generations to redefine the meaning of success and demonstrate how to live a meaningful life in the material world.

For further information about Dan Millman's books and seminars, or to schedule him for a presentation, please visit his website: www.peacefulwarrior.com.

H J Kramer and New World Library are dedicated to
publishing books and audio products
that inspire and challenge us to improve
the quality of our lives and our world.

Our books and audios are available
in bookstores everywhere.
For our catalog, please contact:

H J Kramer/New World Library
14 Pamaron Way
Novato, CA 94949

Phone: (415) 884-2100 or (800) 972-6657
Catalog requests: Ext. 50
Orders: Ext. 52
Fax: (415) 884-2199

Email: escort@newworldlibrary.com
Website: www.newworldlibrary.com